"This book does a tremendous job of describir[...] develop and implement an online science cou[...] face-to-face course. The authors have done an e[...] understanding of the political, theoretical, an[...] [...] online science education."

—*Rob Duncan, Western Governors University*

"Online education has proven itself as a viable alternative for many students. Linda Jeschofnig has been involved in the development of lab science classes for a number of years and now shares her knowledge in this book, a lifeline for colleges and instructors creating online science classes."

—*Cindy Jones, science instructor for CCCOnline and owner, Sagescript Institute*

"I wish *Teaching Lab Science Courses Online* had been available when I started as a resistant faculty member 30 years ago!"

—*Marcia Bradley, professor of science, Ocean County College*

"This book reinforces those who believe in online labs and may change the mind of those who don't."

—*Kimberly F. Regier, Department of Integrative Biology, University of Colorado Denver*

"Linda and Peter Jeschofnig state a compelling argument in support of offering all components of lab-based sciences online, including hands-on lab experiments, and give practical suggestions for doing so. This book is for every serious online science instructor and administrators."

—*Dr. Angie Carraway, chemistry instructor, Meridian Community College*

"A must-read for anyone thinking of teaching an online science course! Even the most experienced online instructors will benefit from the information."

— *Patricia Thompson, professor of chemistry, North Lake College*

"This book discusses the benefit of online education and addresses concerns associated with online science education. Science faculty will be able to design at-home and hands-on laboratory exercises while adhering to high course standards and never compromising the integrity of the course content. This book will benefit every science online instructor and distance education faculty in general."

—*Nahel W. Awadallah, Johnston Community College, director of programs, Humanities, Social, and Natural Sciences*

"*Teaching Lab Science Courses Online* is about learning by doing! It is an eye-opening examination of teaching science successfully in online education."

—*Alanna M. Tynes, professor of biology, Lone Star College-Tomball*

JOSSEY-BASS GUIDES
TO ONLINE TEACHING AND LEARNING

Teaching Lab Science Courses Online

Resources for Best Practices, Tools, and Technology

Linda Jeschofnig
Peter Jeschofnig

JOSSEY-BASS
A Wiley Imprint
www.josseybass.com

Published by Jossey-Bass
A Wiley Imprint
989 Market Street, San Francisco, CA 94103-1741—www.josseybass.com

Library of Congress Cataloging-in-Publication Data

Jeschofnig, Linda, 1948-
    Teaching Lab Science Courses Online : Resources for Best Practices, Tools, and Technology / Linda Jeschofnig and Peter Jeschofnig.
        p.   cm.—(Jossey-Bass Guides to Online Teaching and Learning ; 29)
    Includes bibliographical references and index.
    ISBN 978-0-470-60704-6 (pbk.)
    ISBN 978-1-118-00999-4 (ebk)
    ISBN 978-1-118-01000-6 (ebk)
    ISBN 978-1-118-01001-3 (ebk)
        1. Science—Study and teaching (Higher)   2. Laboratories.   3. Web-based instruction—Design.
4. Science—Electronic information resources.   I. Jeschofnig, Peter.   II. Title.
    Q181.J376 2011
    507.8'5—dc22

                                                                                              2010048702

Printed in the United States of America
FIRST EDITION

PB Printing   10 9 8 7 6 5 4 3 2

CONTENTS

PREFACE

Community, education, business, and government leaders are increasingly recognizing the decline in science literacy in the United States and despairing of the alarming implications such ignorance bodes for the future and progress of the nation, the planet, and humanity. The seriousness of this situation is evidenced by recent presidential initiatives and new funding allocated in support of educating the scientists, engineers, environmentalists, inventors, health care providers, and other science-related professionals to lead the nation in science for the benefit of current and future generations.

There is no doubt that every aspect of modern life stems from scientific advancement and that the future prosperity of our country and the world requires a more science-literate population as well as more and better scientists. It is important that today's students acquire genuine understanding of science and the scientific method if they are to accurately assess cause-and-effect relationships, to address global environmental issues, to succeed in science- and technology-related careers, and to acquire the rational thinking skills needed for effective decision making. Government, industry, and education leaders all acknowledge these needs, and their publications are replete with calls for more and better science instruction at all levels of education.

These experts know that when students study science and follow the scientific method, they cannot help but develop the logical, pragmatic, and critical thinking skills that will serve them well throughout their lives, regardless of their ultimate fields of endeavor. In contrast, a lack of science education and science experimentation opportunities promotes science illiteracy and contributes to a rise in "magical thinking" that impairs the rational decision-making abilities critical to the students' personal success as well as to the success, sustainability, and prosperity of humanity.

THE NEED FOR ONLINE SCIENCE

Over the past decade, the United States has seen a dramatic rise in the online delivery of higher education instruction accompanied by growing evidence of online education's effectiveness. A report from the Sloan Consortium entitled "Staying the Course: Online Education in the United States, 2008" estimates that over 20 percent of all U.S. higher education students were taking at least one online course in the fall of 2007 (Allen & Seaman, 2008). This report also states that the 12.9 percent growth rate for online enrollments far exceeds the 1.2 percent growth of the overall higher education student population.

As online instruction has increasingly become a popular delivery tool for higher education, many have noted and decried the scarcity of laboratory science courses in the online mix of high school and college course offerings. This deficiency has been especially condemned by college students who require laboratory science courses to complete degree and certificate programs or who hope to train in currently lucrative health- and science-related careers but whose complicated lives prevent them from taking courses on campus. The reasons laboratory science courses are thus far infrequently offered online are many, but most revolve around doubts that instruction in laboratory sciences can be effectively delivered online and educators' trepidation about how to provide online students with appropriate experimentation activities that are traditionally associated with effective laboratory science teaching and learning.

The authors of this book are retired college professors who have been recognized as passionate pioneers in the field of distance science education. They so firmly believe in the importance of studying science that they have dedicated their lives to making real-world laboratory science learning experiences available to all students, especially those studying online. Their work in this field along with that of a small core of dedicated online science instructors has proven that the obstacles to teaching laboratory science courses online can be overcome and that students can be genuinely engaged in rigorous science learning from a distance.

To be effective, science education must actively engage students. It must stimulate and foster curiosity and the inquiry skills that drive hypothesis formulation. It must kindle contemplation and creativity to devise tests of hypotheses. Its activities must hone observation, recording, reporting, and analytical skills. And it must demonstrate the importance of correctly accumulating valid evidence and properly evaluating genuine cause-and-effect relationships. These life skills and science learning experiences can be effectively taught online as evidenced by several hundred online science educators we have encountered.

THE PURPOSE OF THIS BOOK

This book examines the obstacles to teaching laboratory sciences online and explores means of overcoming these obstacles. It also describes laboratory science courses that are being effectively taught 100 percent online by a small cadre of experienced educators.

Engaging in laboratory experimentation and following the scientific method is universally recognized as the best way to learn science. The method of course delivery is irrelevant to this science learning requirement. Regardless of how, where, or when a science course is taught, experimentation that follows the scientific method must be a part of the experience. Thus this book explores options available for providing online students with valid science laboratory experiences. These options include computer simulations, remote labs, kitchen science labs, instructor-assembled lab kits, and commercially assembled lab kits.

The topic of online laboratory science education is particularly relevant to the academic deans, training teachers, and curriculum developers who are responsible for creating and delivering online courses. It is also relevant to high school and college science educators who wish to transition to online instruction with off-campus science experimentation activities; to current online science instructors who wish to improve or expand their online science courses; and to home-school parents seeking to make their science instruction more engaging. Specific examples highlighted in this book include the disciplines of anatomy and physiology, biology, chemistry, geology, microbiology, and physics. However, the materials covered also have applicability to astronomy, forensics, environmental science, and other laboratory science subdisciplines.

Economic and societal forces are driving the demand for well-trained online science educators. Today's students want and require greater exposure to lab science courses, and they want these courses to be offered fully online. Many of these students are nontraditional, adult learners who are returning to college to obtain knowledge and skills that match current employment opportunities and who take online courses to accommodate their complicated schedules. Traditional-age college students are also driving the demand for online courses. This younger generation was brought up with technology, is comfortable with asynchronistic communication, and wants the freedom and flexibility of anytime-anywhere education that online courses provide. Both groups are attracted by the savings in time and transportation realized through online education. Military personnel stationed abroad and students in rural communities beyond commuting distance to a college campus are also major consumers of online courses.

The demand for online courses by these varied consumers has created a tipping point for online education, which is fast becoming the primary instructional mode in higher education. Educational institutions have been actively recruiting and vigorously training nonscience instructors to teach online during the past decade as online education has grown in popularity. However, few laboratory scientists have been recruited or trained to teach their courses online due to the prevalent belief that laboratory sciences can only be effectively taught in campus-based facilities. This mistaken belief has created a scarcity of trained online science educators to meet the growing demand for fully online lab science courses. We hope that the evidence presented in this book will convince skeptical science educators that lab science can be effectively taught online and encourage them to offer their courses online.

Thus, another purpose for this book is for use as a training tool to help address and mitigate higher education's current shortage of online science instructors. By sharing the successful pedagogical methods, technological tools, and best practices of experienced online science educators, this book can not only help to train willing and able online science educators but also reduce the time they need to transition their campus-based lab science courses to online. This book addresses the online science educator shortage in these ways:

1. It encourages science educators to teach their lab science courses online because

   - the world needs science-literate populations;
   - online is fast becoming the major instructional delivery mode of the future;
   - there is a desperate need and demand for lab science courses to be taught online; and
   - there is a corresponding need for lab science educators capable of teaching their courses online.

2. It shows skeptical science educators that it is possible for them to safely and effectively provide online students with great science—learning opportunities that include laboratory experiences to help clarify, amplify, enrich, and reinforce science knowledge.

3. It provides science educators with information, tools, encouragement, examples, and inspiration to help them transition their campus-based lab science courses and laboratory sessions to be taught fully online.

THE ORGANIZATION OF THIS BOOK

The first two chapters of this book discuss the need for science education in general and online science education in particular. We review the perceived and actual obstacles that must be overcome when moving a lab science course completely online.

Chapter 3 explores the technological tools such as learning management systems and Web 2.0 tools that facilitate, enrich, and expand the online teaching realm. Chapter 4 reviews the options available for providing a laboratory experience to accompany online science instruction.

Chapter 5 examines the components of an online course and shows how they should be structured for laboratory science courses. A major issue of concern to new online instructors, academic integrity, is thoroughly explored in chapter 6, which also describes numerous tools that can be used to minimize and detect cheating.

Chapter 7 describes how the different types of laboratory options are incorporated into an online science course. Chapter 8 reviews quantitative as well as qualitative data regarding the effectiveness of online lab science courses and provides several examples from institutions that have moved their science courses online, including how Ocean County College adapted its nursing program, and then all its science programs, for fully online course delivery.

In Chapter 9, long-practicing online science educators offer advice for newcomers to online instruction, and Chapter 10 encourages science instructors to cross the chasm and move into the growing world of online laboratory science instruction. The Appendix provides a detailed case study of Ocean County College's need, thought processes, and implementation procedures employed to initiate an online microbiology course.

ACKNOWLEDGMENTS

There are numerous exceptionally dedicated and competent science educators who have greatly enriched our lives with their friendship and whose tremendous knowledge about teaching, science, and online education has enhanced our own. These individuals through their actions as well as their words continually support science education and teaching excellence. We are extremely grateful for their encouragement of our efforts and their commitment to improving science literacy in the world.

Marge Vorndam, biology professor and co-chair of CCCOnline's Science Department, has been Linda's friend, technical advisor, web assistant, and personal mentor in the biological sciences for almost a decade. Marge is the author of LabPaq's biology manuals for science majors (BK-2A and BK-2B). Her professional efforts and commitment to excellence in serving students' needs is boundless. Marge is retired from the Colorado State University at Pueblo but continues to teach online biology courses for CCCOnline.

Paul Vorndam, chemistry professor and co-chair of CCCOnline's Science Department, has been a witty, willing, and cheerful consultant on all things scientific. He has taught chemistry for the Air Force Academy and CCCOnline for over a decade.

Cynthia Alonzo, microbiology professor, gave up a lucrative research career to make a difference in science education. She is the author of LabPaq's microbiology manual and teaches microbiology online for CCCOnline.

Laszlo Vass, the author of most of LabPaq's anatomy and physiology manuals, utilizes his unique theatrical skills to captivate students' interest and motivate them in their very difficult studies toward careers in health care. He teaches anatomy and physiology online for CCCOnline.

Trina Riegel, geology professor, is the author of LabPaq's physical and historical geology manuals. She teaches online geology courses for a number of colleges including CCCOnline and the University of Maryland.

James Brown, microbiology professor and former dean of Ocean County College, New Jersey, has been tireless in proving and convincing others that rigorous science learning can be delivered effectively via fully online course formats. We are especially grateful for the insightful appendix he contributed to this book that details his firsthand experience in fostering a unique online science program and in teaching microbiology in a fully online format.

Penny Perkins-Johnston is an innovative online anatomy and physiology professor at California State University, San Marcos, who has generously shared her enthusiasm as well as expertise in distance science education with us.

We also wish to thank Cindy Jones, Rusty Roe, Kate Lormand, and the numerous other distinguished online science instructors who so generously have shared their time and expertise with us.

ABOUT THE AUTHORS

Retired Colorado Mountain College (CMC) professors Linda and Peter Jeschofnig are the founders of Hands-On-Labs, Inc., which grew out of a unique micro-scale chemistry kit they created for Peter's distance education students in 1994. Today Hands-On Labs produces over a hundred different LabPaqs for various online sciences courses. Linda and Peter are also the founders of the Institute for Excellence in Distance Science Education, a nonprofit organization dedicated to fostering professional development for distance science educators.

Peter holds undergraduate and graduate degrees from West Texas State University and Western State College of Colorado. He also holds a PhD in anthropology from Southern Methodist University and a PhD in adult science education from Colorado State University. He is a CMC Professor Emeritus, a past chair of CMC's Science Department, Colorado's 2001 Distance Educator of the Year, and a double Fulbright Scholar.

Linda holds a BBA from the University of Houston and an MS from Regis University. She is a former CPA who taught accounting, economics, and business courses at CMC where she was recognized as a master teacher. High ethical standards and business acumen have earned her numerous awards. She was honored as an Outstanding Woman in Business by the Denver Business Journal, and her company was named a 2009 Colorado Company to Watch by the Edward Lowe Foundation.

Teaching Lab Science Courses Online

Why Teach Science Online?

We educators universally agree that studying science and participating in science-laboratory activities is vitally important for a myriad of reasons, not the least of which is the economic prosperity inherent in a science-literate population. The dramatic rise in science illiteracy throughout the United States is appalling and certainly does not bode well for the future of the world (Mooney & Kirshenbaum, 2009). Understanding and addressing the potential impact of science-related political issues such as global warming, endangered species, and general environmental degradation requires that the world's citizens possess fundamentally sound scientific knowledge. People cannot make rational and informed decisions about these major issues unless they have a firm foundation in science knowledge, and such knowledge is acquired by actively studying science and engaging in experimental science activities.

All the medical and technological progress of the modern world has evolved from a foundation of scientific knowledge and understanding. The decline in U.S. students' science test scores and the number of science-related PhDs awarded to Americans is definitely alarming (Mooney & Kirshenbaum, 2009) and threatens the future of our nation, its people, and our global neighbors. Society requires a science-savvy population to fill important science-related jobs as well as to create new advances for general health and prosperity. People must be properly educated in the lab sciences to prepare for vital science-related careers in health, industry, energy, the environment, research, and academic fields.

SCIENCE IS INTEGRATIVE

Science is the most integrative of academic disciplines and thus reinforces all learning. The study of science sharpens students' math and language skills through required mathematical computations and written analysis. It also calls upon students' knowledge in other areas of study as a basis for reflection, association, and creating meaning from their science coursework. Beyond teaching specific science concepts, science curriculums expand and sharpen students' basic language and math skills and foster their understanding of the connections among science, themselves, and other fields of knowledge.

Knowledge integration through science primarily stems from traditional laboratory experiences. Performing science experiments requires data to be accumulated, quantified, graphed, and analyzed—tasks that utilize and hone mathematical skills. Keeping laboratory notes during the performance of an experiment and writing a formal laboratory report at its conclusion polish students' mental organization as well as their writing and communication skills. Examining the relevance of experimental reactions and observations requires contemplating the economic, political, social, and historical implications of science-related concepts. These laboratory activities help to integrate and reinforce students' knowledge of other fields along with their knowledge of science.

SCIENCE TEACHES PROBLEM-SOLVING SKILLS

For us, the most important reason to foster an educated population well schooled in laboratory sciences is that experiential science activities teach solid problem-solving and decision-making skills. People who in their science studies have been fully and concretely engaged in the pragmatic approach of the scientific method cannot help but develop sound logic and critical-thinking skills.

Through learning, understanding, and practicing the scientific method again and again and again during their coursework, students are less inclined toward "magical thinking," for they are able to personally grasp and logically correlate genuine cause-and-effect relationships and to be skeptical of unsubstantiated inferences. The critical- and logical-thinking abilities students gain from science-lab experimentation improve their decision-making abilities and will serve them well throughout their lives, even if their future career paths are not science related.

WHY SCIENCE IS NOT OFTEN TAUGHT ONLINE: IT'S THE LAB COMPONENT!

Why Science Courses Are Seldom Offered Online

- Uncertainty about how to offer a valid lab component with online courses
- Difficulty moving outside the box of the campus laboratory experience
- Doubts that students can independently perform lab work in nontraditional places
- Doubts that off-campus lab work can be as effective as formal laboratory work
- Fear about safety and liability issues if students experiment without supervision

All major educational institutions and science associations, including the American Chemical Society (ACS), the College Board, the National Science Foundation (NSF), and the National Science Teachers Association (NTSA), concur that laboratory experiences are vital to learning science. NSTA (2009) states, "For science to be taught properly and effectively, labs must be an integral part of the science curriculum." Science labs have customarily been expected to be tactile, hands-on experiences that require physical manipulations of science equipment and materials. Many people and organizations believe that only tactile experimentation can provide valid lab experiences. The ACS in a position paper on computer simulations in academic laboratories (2009) states quite forcefully that " computer simulations are not a substitute for student hands-on laboratories from the kindergarten level through undergraduate education." This is among the reasons the majority of state education standards require hands-on "wet-lab" experiences to earn accredited and transferable college course credits.

Stereotypically, we science educators tend to be a rather opinionated and contrarian bunch with a slightly mischievous sense of humor. We often enjoy splitting hairs and playing devil's advocate for the sake of a stimulating conversation. However, when it comes to the subject of laboratory experimentation, we universally agree without equivocation that tactile wet-lab experiences are the best way to learn science and are indispensable for genuine science learning.

Because science literacy is so vital to students and society and because experimentation is so vital to learning science, laboratory activities have been a standard component of science curriculums ever since institutions of higher learning were established. For over 200 years, science experimentation has primarily been performed within the formal laboratory facilities of institutional campuses. We science educators have for so long worked inside the box of traditional campus laboratories that it is difficult to for us to believe that real science can be learned and genuine experimentation can be performed anywhere else.

There are numerous ways to provide online students with good science-laboratory experiences. A popular option is hybrid courses where content is offered online but students are required to attend laboratory sessions on campus. Although not highly favored as a complete substitute for tactile laboratory experiences, computer simulations have also been successfully employed by numerous professors, and some believe they provide online students with adequately realistic and sophisticated laboratory experiences (Woodfield et al., 2004). This is especially true for "remote labs," where students, from the comfort of their computer, actually manipulate sophisticated science equipment located in professional laboratories. Several instructors have devised ingenious kitchen-science laboratory experiments that students can perform utilizing simple materials found in the average home or community (Carnevale, 2002). A few instructors design lab experiments that students can perform alone, and they check out laboratory supplies and equipment to them so that they can perform the experiments off campus (Jeschofnig, 2006). There are also commercial companies that produce academically aligned lab kits for purchase and use by online higher education students. All these lab options are currently in use and are explored in further detail later in this book.

Despite evidence to the contrary, many of our fellow instructors remain unconvinced and believe an online science course cannot provide genuinely effective laboratory experiences. Accordingly, some institutions still refuse to grant transfer credits for lab-science courses taught online. Fear that transfer credits may be denied to their students has discouraged many colleges and instructors from exploring effective off-campus laboratory experiences and developing lab-science courses for fully online delivery. This is terribly unfortunate because, as objective studies mentioned throughout this book reflect, effective science-laboratory experiences are definitely achievable by fully online students, and students who acquire undergraduate lab-science credits online have no problem progressing into graduate-level science careers.

WHY SCIENCE EXPERIMENTATION IS IMPORTANT

Why are physical experiments so important to learning science? Why does the act of experimenting provide a better learning experience than one gained from traditional didactic instruction or from reading textual materials or watching videos? Specifically, science experimentation benefits learning via direct, concrete, and personal experience with information. Science experimentation epitomizes the concepts of experiential learning because it employs relevance with activity-based events to convey meaning and understanding (NSEE, 1998).

The very physicality of science experimentation utilizes the physical senses and creates a gut-level of understanding. It promotes an intellectual learning experience that allows the knowledge gained to be absorbed on a variety of physical and mental levels. That is why experiential learning tends to create more profound and longer-lasting knowledge of subject matter than didactic learning, a phenomena confirmed over half a century ago by the National Training Laboratories and illustrated in its learning pyramid (Figure 1.1).

Direct participation in a learning activity, in contrast to passively observing or listening to information, makes the learning personal and paves the way for deeper, more genuine, and longer-lasting comprehension. Unlike passive learning where the instructor provides information with no active engagement by the student, experiential learning is corporeal, active, and requires the student to examine, to touch, to manipulate, to contemplate, and to have physical knowledge of the phenomenon being studied (Cantor, 1996).

In essence, science is the continuing effort to discover and increase human knowledge and understanding through disciplined research, a process encompassed by the scientific method. Science also deals with change—the causes and the effects of change. Through science experimentation, students observe the elements of change firsthand and for themselves. They gain direct, up-close, and personally relevant knowledge of the phenomena they study. The concrete and personal nature of physical exploration provides more weight to knowledge

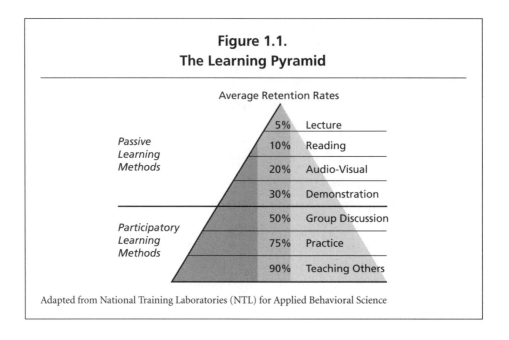

Figure 1.1.
The Learning Pyramid

Average Retention Rates

Passive Learning Methods	5%	Lecture
	10%	Reading
	20%	Audio-Visual
	30%	Demonstration
Participatory Learning Methods	50%	Group Discussion
	75%	Practice
	90%	Teaching Others

Adapted from National Training Laboratories (NTL) for Applied Behavioral Science

so gained. Active science experimentation leads to knowledge, not simply on a shallow informational level, but at a deeper, root level of understanding that provides genuine ownership of the information. That firm foundation of knowledge then opens the door for higher levels of comprehension of related concepts. In 1964 the renowned physicist Richard Feynman related knowledge to experimentation when he stated:

> The test of all knowledge is experiment. Experiment is the sole judge of scientific "truth." But what is the source of knowledge? Where do the laws that are to be tested come from? Experiment, itself, helps to produce these laws, in the sense that it gives us hints. But also needed is imagination to create from these hints the great generalizations—to guess at the wonderful, simple, but very strange patterns beneath them all, and then to experiment to check again whether we made the right guess.

Whenever students burn a cake in the oven or whenever their car refuses to start, they unconsciously begin to practice the scientific method and go through the process of formulating, testing, and revising a hypothesis to determine what went wrong. It is important to help students realize that they already know how to do science and that by taking a lab-science course, they are simply broadening their awareness of the world around them.

Experimentation is essential to the study of science. Online, just as on campus, the laboratory component of a lab science course should be structured in a way that allows students to gain significant personal familiarity with experimental procedures and processes as well as opportunities to participate in designing experiments. Through their lab work, students should come to appreciate the importance of direct observation of science phenomena and learn to distinguish between inferences based on theory and the outcomes of experiments. Further, the laboratory experience should help students develop a broad set of basic skills and tools in science experimentation and data analysis as they learn and master basic science concepts.

A charming, archaic story that well illustrates the importance of science experimentation comes from the renowned scientist Ira Ramsen (1846–1927), who wrote about experiencing a chemical phenomenon when a child:

> While reading a textbook of chemistry, I came upon the statement, "nitric acid acts upon copper" . . . and I [was] determined to see what this meant. Having located some nitric acid . . . I had only to learn what the words "act upon" meant. . . . In the interest of knowledge I was even willing to sacrifice one of the few copper cents then in my possession. I put one of them on the table; opened the bottle marked "nitric acid"; poured some of the liquid on the copper; and prepared to make an observation. But what was this wonderful thing which I beheld? The cent was already changed, and it was not a small change either. A greenish blue liquid foamed and fumed over the cent and the table. The air . . . became colored dark red. . . . How could I stop this? I tried by picking up the cent and throwing it out of the window. . . . I learned another fact; nitric acid . . . acts upon fingers. The pain led to another unpremeditated experiment. I drew my fingers across my trousers and discovered nitric acid acts upon trousers. . . . I tell it even now with interest. It was revelation to me. Plainly the only way to learn about such remarkable kinds of action is to see the results, to experiment, to work in the laboratory. (as cited in Gutman, 1940)

Many of today's scientists claim that experimentation with a favorite childhood toy, a chemistry set, was responsible for their interest in science. This favorite toy of yore has long since disappeared due to government restrictions, safety concerns, and liability issues. Our national decline in science literacy may be partly attributed to the disappearance of these old chemistry sets which sparked the scientific curiosity of prior generations.

Although a large percentage of children in elementary school show high interest and enthusiasm for science classes, they tend to lose that interest and grow to dislike science classes in junior and senior high schools. The students who disliked science in high school often claim that they lost interest because teachers demanded rote memorization and the lessons were not interesting or inspiring and seemed to have no relevance to their lives. Having access to those old chemistry sets may have kept their interest alive (Jeschofnig, 2004).

CHANGE IS HARD

Like us, most science educators have spent years working inside formal campus laboratory settings, but unlike us, they have seldom performed science work anywhere else. They are accustomed to teaching science in a particular way, to using specific science equipment, and to performing experiments in a set, traditional manner. It is understandable that many of our science colleagues have difficulty believing students can learn science in any way other than the way they learned science or that students do not need to work inside a formal campus laboratory setting as they did. An analogy is classroom teaching via lecture. It has been shown to be the least effective method of instruction, yet most traditional instructors of all disciplines continue using it because that is how they were taught.

As distance-teaching methods and online education have evolved, science educators have debated how to provide distant online students with traditional laboratory experiences. Many feel it is an impossible task and refuse to even consider offering science courses online. They believe valid science experimentation can only be performed on campus. Because they see no way to provide campus laboratory experiences to online students who cannot commute to campus, they also see no way to effectively offer accredited science courses online.

Several concerned scientists felt there had to be a way to accommodate online students and enable them to meet traditional laboratory learning objectives. They began trying a multitude of lab options ranging from computer simulations, kitchen chemistry, and hybrid lab sessions to commercial or instructor-assembled home lab kits. As we will later explore, these options have been tried with varying degrees of student success and instructor satisfaction.

MOVING LABS OFF CAMPUS

Even when students are given appropriate experiments and supporting materials, many of our science colleagues still find it difficult to believe students can effectively perform lab experiments completely on their own, in their own homes, without an instructor or a lab assistant watching over them. Although there has been little outside research to date on home-based academic laboratory kits, Hands-On Labs (HOL), the pioneer in this field, has accumulated data from numerous quantitative studies independently conducted by professors across the nation using HOL's commercial lab kits in different science disciplines. These studies consistently report that college students can responsibly and effectively perform rigorous science experiments alone and off campus when given the opportunity and tools to do so. The cumulative data received through 2009 show that first- and second-semester college students using their commercially assembled science-lab kits at home have at least an equal, if not better and more satisfying, learning experience and higher grades than their campus-based peers. Over 92% of those students report making an A (64%) or B (28%) in their lab-science courses (HOL, 2009). Studies of students performing kitchen-lab experiments at home report similar findings (Carnevale, 2002) and confirm students' ability to effectively and independently perform instructional science-laboratory work off campus.

The basis of these results seems to emanate from these details:

- When working off campus, the students must take responsibility for their own learning.

- There is no lab tech, instructor, or fellow student to hold the students' hand and tell them what to expect.

- There is no time limit on how long students can take to fully engage in and understand the results of their experimentation activities.

- It takes a greater investment of personal time and effort to perform experiments independently, and the greater the length of time spent learning, the higher the probability of success.

- Through active engagement with the subject matter, it becomes more personally relevant and interesting to the students.
- The resultant discovery learning is therefore personally gained, wholly owned, and a source of great pride as well as deep understanding.

The following comment from a student at the University of Delaware in response to an article on evidence supporting online education (Jaschik, 2009) identifies rationales for success in online education:

> The self-motivation factor and working at my own pace are two reasons why I believe online learning is more efficient than traditional face to face lecture style learning . . . students don't always come to class prepared or motivated to focus on the material. Whether we are up late the night before from studying, socializing, or various other reasons and find our eyes drooping and minds drifting, or we are thinking about other obligations, once a moment of lecture passes without us taking anything out of it, we can never get that moment back. But with online learning, the course is more flexible to our readiness to focus. Lectures can be read and reread, videos that professors post can be rewound, and everything is automatically stored and can be retrieved easily. Online learning is more convenient for the modern college student and allows us derive the most out of our sometimes limited and unpredictable willingness to focus on our work. (George, 2009)

It is assumed that similarly designed learning experiences as well as similarly equipped science-lab kits could produce results equivalent to those found by formal studies of commercially assembled lab kits. From an academic standpoint, the most important thing about these studies is that they have repeatedly demonstrated that students can independently perform and actually learn important science concepts from science experimentation conducted outside of a campus laboratory. Because students can perform genuine science experimentation activities off campus and still have good learning results, even some of our skeptical friends are beginning to admit that lab science courses can be fully and successfully taught online and that experiences inside a formal campus laboratory are not essential to the learning process.

LEARNING WITH OFF-CAMPUS LABS

Further evidence of the validity of alternative lab-learning experiences is that the students using them have no problem advancing into higher levels of science coursework or adjusting to formal laboratory environments. In fact, many students who began their college careers using commercial lab kits to fulfill their science courses' laboratory requirements are today practicing doctors, nurses, engineers, and even PhD science researchers (Jeschofnig & Spencer, 2008).

Even though performing laboratory experiments independently rather than on campus is much more difficult and time consuming, a study of students using commercially assembled lab kits indicates that they enjoy the challenge and the discovery learning that comes from performing science experiments by themselves instead of as part of a campus group (HOL, 2009). They especially value the savings in time and commuting expense as well as the flexibility of being able to perform their lab-science coursework at a time and place of their own choosing. These advantages seem to outweigh the need to purchase commercial lab kits at an average price that approaches $200, because 71% of the students surveyed felt the price was fair in relationship to the value it provided, and 77% would take another course requiring the purchase of a commercial lab kit (HOL, 2009).

A decade of data acquired from science instructors using commercially assembled lab kits supports the authors' contention that students can perform rigorous, real-world, college-level, wet-lab experimentation at home when given clear instructions and appropriate materials (HOL, 2009). Science instructors need no longer fear that their online students will miss vital laboratory learning experiences just because they can't come to campus. Because it has been repeatedly shown that students in all science disciplines can do genuine science experimentation work off campus, institutions should no longer refuse to offer first- and second-year lab-science courses online for fear that online students will lack hands-on lab learning experiences.

IF EDUCATION'S FUTURE IS ONLINE, LAB SCIENCES MUST BE TAUGHT ONLINE!

There can be little doubt that online instruction is becoming an increasingly important delivery mode for higher education. The past decade has seen online courses rapidly become an integral part of college educational systems, especially at the community college level. The sixth annual report of the Sloan consortium, *Staying the Course: Online Education in the United States, 2008* (Allen & Seaman, 2008), reports that over 3.9 million students took at least one online course during the fall 2007 semester. For the entire 2006–2007 academic year, 12.2 million people enrolled in college-level distance-education courses. This represents a fourfold growth from 2000–2001, when only 3 million were enrolled (Taylor, 2009).

The rapid move to online education is further confirmed by the 2008 Sloan report's comparison of a 12.9% growth rate in online higher education enrollments versus only a 1.2% growth rate in traditional campus enrollments (Allen & Seaman, 2008). These numbers show that higher education students are choosing online courses at ten times the rate they are choosing campus-based courses. In light of this data and historical trends, there can be little doubt that online enrollments will continue to escalate over the next decade and that the demand for online courses will increase long into the future.

The past decade has also seen the arrival of new higher education institutions specifically dedicated to online instruction. CCCOnline was launched in 1998 as one of the first completely online institutions in the nation. This consortium of Colorado community colleges and universities was charged by the state of Colorado with responsibility for ensuring quality in online course delivery throughout state. Its initial 109 enrollments in the spring of 1998 expanded to 14,865 enrollments by the fall of 2009. CCCOnline currently serves over 17,000 students and offers over 1,400 courses annually (CCCOnline, 2008).

Because science education is vitally important to individuals and society, it must be supported and offered in all instructional modes. Online education is undoubtedly a major mode of instruction delivery today and will be an increasingly important mode of instruction delivery in the future. Thus, it is incumbent upon institutions to ensure that lab-science courses are included among the courses available via online instruction. In his statement of support for quality online instruction, Dr. John Ittelson (2009), California State University, Monterey Bay, professor of Information Technology and Communication Design and director of Distributed and Online Learning, makes a compelling argument for moving science education fully online:

> As this country faces massive challenges in economics, global warming, and the environmental and social upheaval that these challenges will surely create, our educational system must rise to the

task of providing an educated population of citizens and leaders who understand the challenges and who can envision the solutions we must implement. The students of today will become those leaders. We need to turn to new models of higher education to meet the needs of this emerging student population.

PERHAPS CAMPUSES ARE PASSÉ

Some authors contend that brick-and-mortar educational institutions may soon be a thing of the past (Teachout, 2009; Lamb, 2009). This claim resonates intuitively as the cost associated with constructing campus facilities and conducting campus classes continues to mount. At the same time both the number of higher education students and the number of students demanding fully online courses are escalating. Ambient Insight's chief research officer, Sam S. Adkins, predicts that by 2014 over half of higher education instruction will occur online (Nagel, 2009).

The demand for online education is primarily student driven. It appears that once students have succeeded in an online course and enjoyed the freedom and flexibility it provides, personal preference as well as economic necessity drive them to take additional courses online (Lamb, 2009). However, the Sloan report (Allen & Seaman, 2008) indicates that the proportion of institutions believing online course delivery should be a critical element in their long-term institutional strategy has incongruently leveled off. This obvious gap between students' growing demand for online education and institutions' desire and ability to provide online courses must be quickly addressed.

Why Now Is the Time for Online Courses

The dramatic rise in demand for online courses is not surprising when one considers the confluence of several factors:

- Substantial declines in the cost of computer technology and corresponding increases in computer ownership
- The continuing rise in computer literacy among the general population
- The coming of age of highly computer-savvy generations
- Improvements in and global dissemination of access to high-speed broadband technology

- Continuous improvements in the quality, features, and user-friendliness of online learning-management systems for both instructors and students
- Increasing availability of quality online teaching and learning resources, including new Web 2.0 communication and collaboration tools
- Dramatic declines in states' and institutions' financial resources to stock, staff, and maintain undergraduate laboratory facilities
- Lack of institutional resources to build additional campuses, classrooms, and laboratory facilities to accommodate growing enrollments
- Increasing time, costs, and inconvenience associated with commuting to a college campus
- Increasing student demand for the convenience and flexibility of anytime-anywhere courses

Who's Not Coming to Campus

A substantial portion of the demand for online courses comes from nontraditional students who require online courses to accommodate schedules complicated by work commitments and family obligations. Most adults' work schedules cannot accommodate being on campus for the 9 to 12 hours per week required by a typical lab science course, and their schedules usually conflict with assigned class periods. Older students start or return to college for knowledge and skills that match their employment opportunities. They tend to be more mature, focused, responsible, and capable of working independently.

Adult women are a substantial number of online course consumers. They seek out online lab science courses and constitute over 70% of commercial science-kit purchasers (HOL, 2009). The vast majority of these women work outside their home or have small children and simply cannot attend campus classes. The increasing availability of online courses in various disciplines is making it possible for this previously underserved population to take control of their lives, complete their degrees, achieve their career goals, and improve the economic welfare of their families.

High unemployment rates and a downturned economy are also driving the demand for online courses. Laid-off and soon-to-be laid-off workers return to college in droves for retraining in fields of predicted future employment. Most of these fields are science related, such as health care, green energy, and environmental technology. Ironically, the same economic factors driving demand for higher education are also making it more difficult for colleges to satisfy that demand; instead, many are being forced by budget cuts to offer fewer campus-based classes. However, those institutions with the existing infrastructure to offer online courses and programs are finding themselves poised to reap the related benefits of increased enrollments.

Traditional-age and even full-time and campus-based college students are also driving the demand for online courses. Raised on technology, this generation is comfortable with asynchronistic methods of communication and with interacting in online and telecommunication formats. Most institutions require at least two, and often four, semesters of science instruction for their degree programs. Although many students could take these science courses on campus, they often find the campus version of the course is full or its timing, especially that of lab sessions, conflicts with their other courses or commitments. Thus, the availability of online courses benefits even on-campus students for it allows them to complete their coursework and to graduate within their expected timeframe.

Online courses also tend to better accommodate different learning and social styles. Unlike the traditional lecture methods of instruction practiced on most campuses, online courses allow the students to structure and approach the course materials in ways that fit the way they best learn. Shy students who are too timid to speak up and contribute to campus classroom discussions often find their voices when participating in required online discussion boards and benefit greatly from the availability of online classes. The asynchronistic nature of online discussions allows them ample time to frame their comments, avoid the pressure of a live audience, and genuinely feel they are part of the class.

Other major consumers of online courses are military personnel stationed abroad and even those stationed stateside because most of them face the prospect of being deployed abroad at any time. Instead of having to drop campus-based courses, soldiers can continue and complete online courses regardless of where they may be reassigned. Other online-course consumers include rural students, international students, and students who live beyond a reasonable commuting distance to campus. These various groups share a need for lab-science courses as a part of their degree and training programs and all are attracted to the flexibility and transportation-related savings that online education provides.

All the above factors increase the need and demand for online education. The evolution of online education into a primary instructional mode, combined with the need for improved science education, requires that lab-science courses be included in the mix of courses offered fully online.

The welfare of the world requires improved science literacy, and the related socioeconomic factors require educational institutions to design and provide lab-science courses that are delivered fully online. To meet this responsibility, higher education institutions must encourage, train, and equip adequate numbers of science educators to transition their lab-science courses from strictly campus formats into formats that can be taught fully online.

Teaching Science: Online Versus Face to Face

In many ways, there are no differences between the way science educators teach science online and the way they teach it face-to-face (F2F) on campus. The same course content is covered, the same homework is assigned, and the same types of quizzes, lab assignments, and exams are given. But that is where the similarities end.

I CAN'T SEE YOU

An obvious difference between online and on-campus courses is that there is no corporal student body to observe in an online class. Instructors may never see their online students in person and may never hear them speak. There is no body language to observe and read and no vocal intonation to convey meaning. On campus it is possible to look around the classroom or lecture hall to observe students' faces for the purpose of divining whether they've understood salient points, but it is not that easy with online classes.

The above is true for both science and nonscience courses. However, science primarily deals with problem solving. Not being able to physically observe and interact with students can be a hindrance to science instructors, who need to gauge how well students are following a problem-solving process. It is not possible to see the illumination on students' faces when light bulbs of understanding are turned on or to observe the wrinkled brows and perplexed looks of complete incomprehension. Instead, online science instructors have to prod students to tell them when something is amiss, and they must be extra sensitive to verbal clues of comprehension or confusion in students' lab reports, discussion board comments, and exam papers.

ONLINE COMMUNICATION IS DIFFERENT

Yes, online science instructors can and do often have video conferences with their students. Improvements in technology are continuously making this easier and more feasible, but seeing and being seen by a student via a broadcast is not as powerful as a live interaction. Science instructors can also have telephone conferences with their students. Communicating over the telephone is easier and faster than typing a letter or an e-mail, but phone calls also have their limitations.

The bottom line is that preferred one-on-one and F2F live communication with online students is generally not possible. The primary means of communication between online instructors and their students is via the written word. This requires science educators to carefully choose their words, craft their sentences, and polish their diagrams and illustrations in an attempt to communicate as clearly and precisely as possible and minimize misunderstandings. This is often the most time-consuming process for online educators. Yet, just as students benefit from being forced to organize their thoughts by putting them in writing, instructors do too. Effective online science educators save time by saving and organizing their best illustrations and responses to frequently asked questions so they are readily available for quick personal tailoring. Thus these instructors do not need to reinvent the wheel each semester by compiling new responses to typical questions for multiple students.

ONLINE COMMUNICATION IS DELAYED

New online-science instructors often worry about the time lag in responding to students' questions and in receiving students' responses to their questions. They fear this delay may be an impediment to students' learning. However, asynchronistic communication is the nature of online instruction, which, like all forms of communication, has its pros and cons. Some contend that asynchronistic communication actually helps to improve the quality of communication because there is an interval for careful thought and consideration before a response is compiled and presented. Further, asynchronistic communication forces improvement in the long-term memories and focusing abilities of the communicators.

Experienced online educators usually come to regard the delays inherent in asynchronistic courses to benefit their students, and this is especially true for science. The simple fact that the instructor is not immediately available to answer questions gives students the time and opportunity to seriously contemplate their questions and to possibly arrive at their own answers. Further, the act of having to phrase questions in coherent text helps students clarify the issues for themselves. While waiting for feedback from an instructor, science students will usually develop the answer for themselves by thinking through the question, conferring with colleagues on a discussion board, or performing online research or laboratory experimentation. Just as teaching reinforces learning, the opportunity for students to answer each others' questions contributes to their comprehension. All these activities contribute to a discovery-learning experience that is much deeper, longer lasting, and personally satisfying to students (Chenobu, 2007; Vorndam, 2007).

ONLINE COMMUNICATION IS MEANINGFUL

Instructors new to online teaching fear they will lose the ability to create meaningful relationships with their students. Interestingly, once they have a little online teaching experience under their belt, they usually find their relationships with their online students are closer and more meaningful than their relationships with their on campus students. Perhaps this is because online lab-science classes involve more extensive and direct communications, and this communication between instructors and students is more deliberate and purposeful and thus more meaningful.

Discussion boards are among the most important elements in the structure of online courses. It is a best practice for lab-science courses to have two discussion boards, one dedicated strictly to the labs and the other to the course content. Discussion boards serve a multitude of purposes:

- They allow students and the instructor to come to know each other very well.

- They provide a forum for discussion of posted questions, course concepts, and problem issues.

- They are also a place where students can seek help, share information, offer help, and present their personal views on a topic.

Best practices require that substantial participation in discussion boards be a major component of the course and students' final grades. Students are thus forced to participate and cannot hide in the back of the class or behind their keyboards. It is through observing and participating in the conversations on discussion boards that science instructors get to genuinely know their students, to judge their progress in the course, and to evaluate their comprehension of course content and assignments.

Instructors frequently express amazement at the quantity and the quality of their interactions with their online students. Despite never or rarely seeing each other face to face, both students and instructors report higher levels of personal satisfaction with their online course interactions than with their campus-based course interactions. Perhaps online interactions seem more intimate and personally relevant because instructors and students directly address and directly respond to each other. Personally interacting with an instructor makes a student feel like a unique, thinking individual instead of just another student in a sea of faces. Similarly, the instructor senses that he or she is making more of an impact on each individual student's life, for that truly is the case.

The typical online lab-science course's enrollment is usually limited to between 20 and 30 students, with an average of around 25 students. This is on par with the average size of most community college courses. However, such small class sizes are in substantial contrast to typical four-year college and university courses that are often conducted in classrooms with upward of 50 students or in large lecture halls of several hundred students.

WHERE IS THE LAB?

Of course, the biggest difference between a lab-science course online and on campus is the location of the laboratory. Online students perform their lab work individually and off campus instead of in groups and on campus. This is not necessarily a bad thing.

Far too many higher education institutions lack adequate brick-and-mortar laboratory facilities for their undergraduate students to have sufficient time and space for in-depth science experimentation. On-campus laboratory experiments must too often be performed within large groups of students, in overcrowded facilities, and under severe time constraints. Although performing hands-on labs is the best way to learn science, sadly, few campus-based students have adequate hands-on opportunities in their campus-based labs. Usually only the brightest or most assertive students are allowed to perform the experimental procedures.

The others in the lab groups are too often relegated to watching and thus have a passive and impoverished learning experience.

The most common feedback from college students performing their science-lab experiments at home relates to how much they enjoy being able to perform the labs themselves and having adequate time to complete the experiments and fully understand what they are doing. They often report, "I got to do every step of every lab myself" as though performing laboratory experiments is a unique privilege (HOL, 2009). Freeing students from the time and place constraints of typical campus laboratories allows them to become more intimately engaged in the science learning experience (Chenobu, 2007).

The privacy of an off-campus environment also gives science students the opportunity to fully concentrate on what they are doing without being rushed or intimidated by faster students or by impatient lab assistants. They are not stifled by concerns about what other students may be thinking, and they have the luxury of taking their time to truly understand the concepts they are investigating. Without lab partners, instructors, or lab assistants to hold their hand, tell them what to expect, and explain what their observations mean, students must perform and experience the experiments themselves. It is thus no surprise that both online instructors and students find that off-campus laboratory experiences provide students with a greater depth of science learning and personal satisfaction (Vorndam, 2007).

TECHNOLOGY MAKES IT POSSIBLE

It is not necessary to be a technology junkie or a cyber geek to teach online. However, the instructor needs to be open to the ways technology can enhance online course delivery and to be willing to invest time to master specific computer programs commonly used online. In addition to the software related to the learning management system (LMS) that hosts the course content (which will be discussed later), instructors must be able to use standard word-processing and spreadsheet software; be able to send and receive e-mail; and know how to download, upload, and attach communication documents. These are the basic tools of online communication, and effective communication is paramount to online instruction's success.

There is a learning curve in becoming familiar with each institution's LMS platform that hosts online courses. However, it is a small learning curve because today's LMSs are genuinely user friendly to the point that inputting specific course materials and utilizing their various tools almost seem intuitive. The purpose of this book is not to teach instructors how to use LMS technology, but it will later show how LMS technology can be used in specific ways to enhance an online lab-science course. Numerous LMS tutorials are available to walk a novice through the basics, and online instructors are usually delighted to share information and talk about the features they have found most helpful.

Chapter 3 contains summary information about popular technological tools and discusses how they can be used with online instruction. The list is not exhaustive because the objective of this book is not to provide detailed instruction in the use of technology. Rather, the information in Chapter 3 is provided to illustrate how current technology can be used to enhance an online lab-science course.

There are numerous technical bells and whistles available to add whiz-bang features to an online course's content. Nevertheless, all the basic technology an instructor needs in order to create and teach an effective lab-science course online is contained in the typical LMS. Online science instructors should try to keep abreast of the technological tools of their trade and to explore those that promise to enhance their communication with students and their students' learning. However, the most important thing to remember is that although new computer technologies may merit exploration and possible integration into a course, they are not absolutely necessary. The quality of instructor and student interactions is much more important than the technology that channels their communications.

OVERCOMING OBSTACLES TO TEACHING SCIENCE ONLINE

What are the factors that deter faculty or institutions from offering online lab-science courses? We have already introduced the primary factor of how to provide traditional laboratory experiences. Beyond the laboratory component, there are legitimate time, resource, and political factors to consider.

It's a Matter of Time

A major concern of lab-science faculty contemplating placing their courses online is the amount of time required to learn the LMS technology and to convert their F2F course materials into online formats (Chisholm, 2006). Most science instructors teach the same courses semester after semester and have well-established presentation methods and materials that they do not relish having to revise or redesign for online delivery.

Similarly, shifting courses online requires institutions to adapt course elements into online formats and train faculty to use technology in a way that facilitates pedagogy (Mishra & Koehler, 2006). However, institutions and new online educators do not need to completely reinvent the wheel because simple course-transfer models are readily available. Pioneering faculty, educational researchers, and technology experts have already laid the groundwork and developed models that facilitate converting F2F courses into online versions without spending days searching for appropriate technology or wasting time using trial and error. The fierce competition among LSM providers ensures that the latest instructional models are annually incorporated into their continuously evolving and improving LMS platforms. Yet there is no denying that both institutions and science instructors must initially invest time and resources into designing their online science courses and inputting their content into the LMS. However, the arduousness of this task diminishes with practice and LMS improvements.

Another concern regarding time is uncertainty about the actual amount of time required to conduct an online science course. This can be substantial or minimal depending upon the science instructor's organization skills, work style, and comfort with technology. Over 85% of faculty with online-course-development experience said it takes "somewhat more" or "a lot more" effort to teach a comparable course online than face to face (Allen & Seaman, 2008). However, considerable time can be saved during the semester because of not having to prepare for lectures; that chore was undertaken during the development and pre-semester stages. Also, no time need be spent commuting to campus lecture halls and laboratories because the course content is online and the students perform lab work on their own. Time is still required to grade assignments, but this task can be streamlined and possibly even avoided through efficient use of the LMS's assessment design and grading tools.

The biggest portion of an online science instructor's time is spent interacting with students: responding to their questions, participating with them in discussion boards, and facilitating their exploration and learning of the course materials. Online instructors continuously interact with students and exchange communication with them numerous times each week, if not each day. This may explain why educators often feel they have closer relationships with their online students than with the ones in their campus classrooms.

The following posting from an F2F and online professor in response to an article supporting online education (Jaschik, 2009) shows the ebb and flow of a typical online course plus the instructor's related time commitments during the term:

> Yes, I may have to spend a little extra time at the beginning of the term making sure my students understand how to navigate the LMS and point them to the online course resources . . . , but they don't get the option of NOT learning how to use them. . . . The results are always the same:
>
> 1. An early steep learning curve, with a fair amount of "I can't" . . .
>
> 2. A period of "Well yeah, maybe I can" when a lot of the tech-forward students start helping their tech-phobic classmates. . . .
>
> 3. What I like to call "the quiet time" from about three weeks into the term until near the end, when my students have finally accepted that I am NOT going to do this for them. . . . "All" I have to do during this period is put out tech brush-fires . . . and serve as guide on the side, spending parts of each class meeting as a "cheerleader," answering questions, doing demonstrations, . . . or just listening to discussions, advising on group projects, and of course my "real job": assessing learning (A LOT) with regular online quizzes and exams. . . .
>
> 4. And lastly, what I term the celebratory "We did it!!!" phase, when the students look up, realize the term is almost over and that they have . . . learned a great deal and that they did it (mostly) all THEMSELVES. (SL, 2009)

Institutions are also concerned about the time investment required to offer online lab-science courses. They fear distracting and diverting the limited time of their limited professional staff for online course development. This time needs to be properly allocated and incorporated into the institution's plans and budgets, but few institutions are able to estimate how long it takes to develop and bring a course fully online, especially an online science course that includes labs.

Fortunately, science faculty members at Ocean County College (OCC) in New Jersey have moved 14 lab-science courses into fully online delivery and have pooled their extensive experiences to create the helpful model shown in

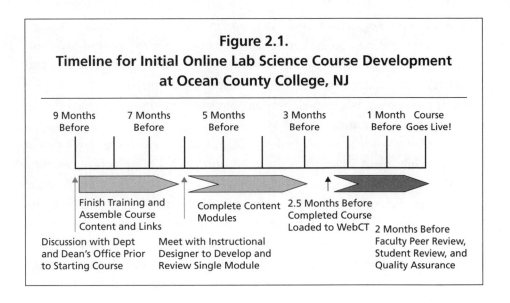

Figure 2.1.
Timeline for Initial Online Lab Science Course Development at Ocean County College, NJ

9 Months Before | 7 Months Before | 5 Months Before | 3 Months Before | 1 Month Before | Course Goes Live!

Finish Training and Assemble Course Content and Links

Complete Content Modules

2.5 Months Before Completed Course Loaded to WebCT

Discussion with Dept and Dean's Office Prior to Starting Course

Meet with Instructional Designer to Develop and Review Single Module

2 Months Before Faculty Peer Review, Student Review, and Quality Assurance

Figure 2.1 (Brown, 2009a). OCC's experiences reflect that for an instructor who is completely new to online, it can take up to nine months to move a lab science course from initial idea to online delivery. However, this process may require substantially less time under different circumstances, at other institutions, and for more experienced online instructors. At institutions with a well-established online culture and extensive online-course-development resources and experience such as CCCOnline, a lab-science course can often be prepared for online delivery in 60 days or less (Vorndam to L. Jeschofnig, personal communication, August 29, 2009).

OCC's nine-month period begins with presenting the initial idea to offer a course online. Then it proceeds through administration buy-in, instructor training, instructional design, development of content modules, uploading the course materials into the LMS, and finally student and faculty QA reviews before the course is actually delivered online to students. See the Appendix for a detailed description of putting a microbiology course online at OCC.

Gaining buy-ins from deans, department chairs, and influential faculty is sometimes the most difficult step, depending upon the institution's political climate and attitudes toward online classes. If the institution already offers online courses, it will have established foundational resources such as a basic online-teacher-training program, an LMS platform, and experienced instructional design and technology staff to assist in the online course development. Although it is possible to offer an online course with free open resources instead of a commercial LMS platform, this requires substantially more computer knowledge and initiative as well as development time on the part of the instructor. For the purposes of this book, it is assumed that commercial online resources are already in place at instructors' institutions.

After receiving approval, the majority of an instructor's course-development time is usually spent learning to use the institution's LMS platform, working with the instructional designer to develop course modules, and compiling the desired course content, including multimedia elements. Then the content and course modules must be loaded into the LMS and its components customized to fit the course design. Finally, the course should be quality reviewed by peers and students. Like all new courses, it may require a bit of tweaking over the first semester or two as the instructor observes what works well for the students and what does not.

It's a Matter of Transfer Credits

All instructors and institutions certainly want their students to have valid and meaningful learning experiences. And no instructors or institutions want their students to be denied transfer credits for academic science work performed under their tutelage.

Due to the much deeper learning experienced via tactile science experimentation, most academic institutions and professional schools, especially nursing and medical schools, will not offer traditional science courses without a wet-laboratory component. For the same reasons, some colleges and universities will not accept the transfer of science course credits if the course did not include a hands-on laboratory component. Similarly, the American Chemical Society recommends that "academic transcripts should clearly disclose whether a chemical laboratory course is hands-on or simulated" (ACS, 2009).

To ensure transferability, both instructors and institutions must determine an effective way to ensure that their online lab-science students have ample and effective laboratory learning opportunities. Doing so both supports their science course objectives and allows the science credits thereby earned to be transferred to other institutions. This is extremely important to students who may wish to continue their higher education at a different institution in the future.

It's a Matter of Politics

For over a decade Hands-On Labs (HOL) has been working to break down the resistance to online science by proving that students can, in fact, perform rigorous, college-level science experimentation work independently and outside of a formal laboratory facility. Its experiences and data long ago established that when given the opportunity, independent students can successfully conduct college-level science experiments at home and in other off-campus locations. Despite this evidence, institutions still experience substantial resistance, especially from long-term and full time faculty. Much of this resistance can be attributed to both insecurity and security issues because some lab-science instructors may feel uncertain about their ability to teach online and fear their jobs may be in jeopardy if they do not want to teach online. Of the institutions surveyed for the *Managing Online Education Programs* study, over 65% cited "faculty resistance" as a major impediment to expanding their online efforts (Green, 2009).

Most institutions want to offer sections of their lab-science courses online, but their bottom-up administrative structures present numerous roadblocks and hurdles that must first be overcome. Traditional academia tends to be fairly egalitarian and to operate via a web of committees that value inclusiveness and consensus building. This is wonderful as long as all minds are thinking alike and time is not of the essence, but this is an age when institutions face budget crises and see campus enrollments declining in favor of online enrollments. Institutions that do not quickly move courses online risk losing enrollment to those that do. There is no time for the luxury of "herding cats." Time normally spent allowing everyone to have a voice, engaging in long debates, and appeasing obstructionists should instead be spent ensuring the quality of online content and delivery systems for needed online lab-science courses.

For all these reasons, many institutions have established separate departments for distance and online education. These reasons also explain the rather rapid success of emerging online-only public and commercial institutions. The top-down management style of such organizations helps speed up online course approval and development processes.

There should be no debate about the effectiveness of online instruction because that has been repeatedly verified (Means, Toyama, Murphy, Bakla, & Jones, 2009). Rather, the debate should be about how to ensure top quality and effectiveness for an institution's online courses and how to encourage and train top faculty to teach online courses or how to acquire excellent adjunct online faculty. However, a top-down style of management in academia can create problems. If an administration forces the adoption of online programs before bringing the majority of instructional faculty fully on board, the resultant internal conflicts can doom their success.

It's a Matter of Confidence

It is also difficult for some educators, especially those who have been around for a long time, to accept the fact that instructors' roles are changing. Instructors entrenched in traditional modes of education cannot imagine students learning science any way other than the way they learned science. But the reality is that students can learn in multiple ways, and they need instructors willing to guide them on their educational journeys. Students gain knowledge by being deliberately directed to engage thoughtfully and constructively with the materials to be learned. The modern science instructor's role is that of a coach who facilitates students' learning by organizing relevant materials, presenting potential paths of inquiry, and posing questions that spark interest, curiosity, investigation, and learning connections. Such facilitation allows students to experience and discover for themselves the basis of science concepts and to gain personal understanding of their relevance and meaning.

Long-standing instructors often have difficulty viewing themselves in this way. They come from a tradition of lecturing professors who pride themselves on developing and delivering standard lectures in their areas of expertise, so they may have difficulty seeing themselves in a different role. It is important that such educators continue to feel valued because their knowledge and experiences are still vitally important to students and society. They must be helped to recognize that the same talents and intelligence that allowed them to acquire their expertise and develop their lectures will also allow them to employ these skills in different ways if they try. Like anything new, there will be a period of adjustment, but we have never met a science professor who has given up online teaching after having tried it.

It's a Matter of Money

As noted earlier, it can take a substantial amount of time to develop an online course, depending upon the experience levels of the instructor and the institution. Developing an online course also requires the input of technical and instructional design staff as well as the provision of course content by an instructor, uploading of the content into an LMS platform by a specialist, and quality testing by students and peers. All these steps, personnel, and related equipment and materials come with a cost and impact an institution's budget.

Institutions have seen the cost of LMS platforms escalate dramatically over the past several years. The LMS industry began with many players engaged in fierce competition via product upgrades and innovation. Yet it has recently been more engaged in fierce business acquisitions and mergers and as a result there are now relatively few players to compete. The resultant increasing cost of LMS platforms contributes to institutions' budgetary woes. Some open-source LMS platforms such as Moodle have arisen, but implementing free LMS software can cost as much as if not more than buying a commercial LMS platform due to the need for substantially more internal IT consulting and support staff.

Beyond the LMS platform's cost, institutions must also invest in campus servers or outside service providers to host online courses in addition to licenses for campus-wide supporting software and teaching tools. The trade-off is to either provide high-quality technology tools or risk losing student enrollment to other institutions that showcase them.

Additional expenditures are also required to hire or pay instructors to develop existing courses for online delivery. Although adjunct instructors can be hired for less than full-time, benefited faculty, online course enrollments are usually limited to around 25 students, so several adjunct lab science instructors may be needed to handle the same number of students that one instructor could reach in a large lecture hall. However, these costs are often offset by savings from not having to stock, staff, insure, and maintain formal science classrooms and laboratory facilities.

It's a Matter of Liability

Institutions and instructors have been well indoctrinated by risk management specialists over the past few decades and are justifiably very cautious. Thus it is no surprise that liability issues tend to be among the first thing they worry about when considering the possibility of offering lab-science courses online with a home laboratory component. They fear that students will not experiment safely off campus and without instructor supervision; that students will hurt themselves or others and damage property; and that those students will sue the instructor or the institution.

Undoubtedly, we live in a litigious society, where there is always the possibility of being sued, justifiably or not. However, liability protection for both instructors and institutions offering online lab-science courses can be achieved and enhanced via repeated and interwoven layers of liability wavers, reinforcing safety instructions, and ample cautions built into both registration and instructional materials. With the help of their legal advisors, institutions can make the provision of a student liability waiver a precondition for enrollment in their online lab-science courses. Notice of this requirement must be prominently published by the institution to ensure students are well aware of it before they enroll in an online lab-science course. The following is an example of such a notice:

> Independent science laboratory experimentation is a requirement of this online course. The nature of science experimentation can involve inherent dangers and requires utmost attention to safety issues. Since students' independent experimentation activities cannot be controlled, a specific precondition of enrolling in this lab science course is that students indemnify the instructor and the institution against any and all liability related to the online student's experimentation activities. The student agrees to fully read, understand, and follow all provided safety instructions prior to beginning an experiment, to experiment only in a safe and responsible manner, to store experimentation materials safely out of the reach of small children, and to fully accept all responsibility for his or her experimental activities related to this online lab science course. (From the Chemistry I syllabus of Dr. Peter Jeschofnig)

A formal liability waiver indemnifying the instructor and institution, and preferably drawn by an attorney, should be signed by each student and submitted to the online instructor before the first lab assignment is due. Lab safety instructions and cautions should be fully outlined in the course materials and continually referenced and repeated throughout the semester. Students tend to be very cautious when they understand that they will be performing real science and must take full responsibility for their own actions. HOL attributes the over-16-year, 100% safety record of its commercial science kits to a combination of all these measures, which continuously reinforce safety, remind online students they are working with potentially hazardous materials, and emphasize their responsibility for the safety of themselves and others.

One reason commercial science-lab kits are often adopted for online courses is that the commercial kit providers usually carry a commercial liability insurance policy that indemnifies the institutions and instructors as well as the company. An institution should make certain a selected provider carries a substantial general liability policy and is willing to provide a certificate of insurance verifying the extent of its coverage and the inclusion of indemnification for the adopting institutions and instructors as well as itself.

It's a Matter of Belief

Who can do something well when they do not believe in what they are doing? Belief in the ability to teach and learn lab sciences in an online format is paramount to being an effective online science educator. No instructor should ever undertake teaching an online course, or for that matter any type of course, without the confidence that he or she, the course materials, and the course-delivery medium can provide an effective learning experience to students. There is growing evidence supporting online instruction as a highly effective medium for education delivery (Frederickson, Reed, & Clifford, 2005; Shachar & Neumann, 2010; Jang, Hwang, Park, Kim, & Kim, 2005; Means et. al., 2009; Mentzer, Cryan, & Teclehaimanot, 2007). The much-discussed and debated 2009 meta-analysis of online learning studies performed for the U.S. Department of Education found that "on average, students in online learning conditions performed better than those receiving face-to-face instruction" (Means et. al., 2009). Yet, there are still many educators who have not been broadly exposed to this information or who continue to adamantly doubt that any online course can be conducted as successfully as a campus-based course.

As with online education in general, the effectiveness of online lab science courses has also been validated, albeit by individual college instructors rather than national surveys. Pioneering science educators who have taken their courses fully online using HOL commercial lab kits have conducted numerous internal and comparative studies to assess the validity of their online students' learning for themselves and their institutions. The data they acquired has been included in professional presentations at many educational conferences across the nation comparing F2F and online course learning outcomes. (Chenobu, 2007; Duncan, 2009; Gibson-Brown, 2010; Herzog, 2008; CCCOnLine, 2008; Jeschofnig, 2009; Perkins-Johnston, 2010; Thompson, 2010; Vass, 2007; Vorndam, 2007). As part of their study, each instructor held constant their course content, exams, lab assignments, and grading rubrics. Several instructors also utilized pre- and post-national science standard exams as benchmarks to confirm student learning. These instructors from different institutions and different science disciplines each arrived at the same conclusion: Their online lab science students perform as well as, and usually better than, their F2F students.

Science instructors must be open to the process and willing to put into their online courses the same level of passion and enthusiasm for teaching they bring to their on-campus courses. As with all new endeavors, there will be a learning curve plus a zone-of-comfort curve and a few stumbling blocks along the way. Yet, as long as science educators believe in themselves, have the best interest of their students in mind, and are genuinely willing to work at the process, there is no reason their online lab science classes should not be successful and satisfying to all.

Enthusiasm for science education and concern for students are paramount to the success of any online lab science course. Instructors who genuinely want to help students learn will communicate that desire as they strive to structure materials and respond to questions in ways that facilitate their students' learning. Such dedicated and innovative instructors were among those who pioneered taking lab science courses online. They recognize the need and importance of serving off-campus students and were determined to provide them with quality instruction via this new medium. No doubt those trendsetters' enthusiasm for education was a driving force behind the accumulated successes in online lab science instruction.

It's a Matter of Being There

As previously discussed, an effective online educator must be willing to invest the upfront time required prior to the semester to design, develop, and organize course materials and to upload them into the LMS. Thereafter, a further time commitment is required to provide online office hours and to frequently access the course's LMS. This is the time when students' direct questions are answered, when the course and lab discussion boards are monitored, and when assignments, thoughts, suggestions, course information, and the instructors' new queries are posted.

Online instructors must also sometimes reach out to help and motivate individual students. For students who do not adequately check into the course or fall behind in their assignments, a phone call or personal e-mail from a concerned instructor can make a profound difference and help get them back on track.

Online classes provide instructors with opportunities to be the kind of teacher they always wished they had had as students, the kind who genuinely care about students and who want to help them learn what they need to know. Online students often state that the single most important factor to their success in their online course was their "instructor's accessibility and commitment to their success" (Carnevale, 2002).

Knowing that their instructor is frequently monitoring their course gives students confidence and motivates them to work harder. Instructors should give students a general idea about the times when they plan to be online as well as set "office" hours when students can count on definitely reaching them online or otherwise. This helps students structure their own time. Online science instructors do not need be tied to a computer every hour of every day of the term, but they should advise students in advance of the times when they will definitely not be available, such as "I'm attending a conference on Wednesday and will be offline the entire day."

Dedicated online science instructors go online and check their courses almost every day of the week. Although frequent checking in during the week is expected, whether instructors should check in over the weekends is up to them. Many choose to go online on weekends because there will be fewer items on Monday awaiting their immediate attention or responses. Similarly, many instructors check their courses several times a day because they prefer to interact with their courses and students in several shorter sessions rather than in one longer one. However, for adjunct instructors with full-time day jobs, going online in the evening may be their only option. The exact timing or frequency of when an instructor is online is not as important as making certain their students are aware of their schedule and letting students know when they can and cannot count on their instructor's help.

Today's students tend to be heavily involved with social networking and continuously interacting with their peers, so they often have unrealistic expectations about how quickly an instructor should respond to them. Although it is important to be accessible to students, it is also important that students understand and respect the fact that their instructor will not be available to them 24/7. This is best done by setting online office hours and making students aware of the instructor's schedule.

An effective online instructor will also need to invest adequate time to ensure all of his or her students are actively engaged in the course. This means frequently reviewing assignment submittals and students' posting to discussion boards so that any laggards can be quickly spotted and encouraged to catch up. Students should not be allowed to fall behind in their coursework or in their discussion board interactions, which are learning activities in themselves. Online course assignments tend to be rather fast-paced, so students who fall a week or more behind in their assignments will usually have great difficulty catching up. Online instructors must be willing to make time to reach out, directly engage, and prod less active students to ensure they contribute.

It's a Matter of Communicating Clearly

To genuinely be effective, online educators should continuously put themselves in the shoes of their students. They must think about what information their students need, and they must then provide it in clear, concise, and precise prose and graphics. Information should be phrased and presented in different ways to accommodate different learning styles. Use bullets to separate and emphasize important points. Boldface or underline important words. Use concrete examples to demonstrate meaning and intent. Use great graphics to convey meaning. Because there is no intonation or body language to assist students in interpreting the instructor's intent, it is the instructor's responsibility to fully and clearly communicate information and be sure that the students have correctly understood their meaning.

In all science courses, there are specific concepts that tend to pose universal difficulty for students trying to learn them. Science instructors should know the common stumbling blocks in their disciplines and provide special guidance, warnings, and information in advance to prevent students from faltering in these areas. For example, chemistry students often have problems with stoichiometry and molecular geometry; physics students usually have difficulty with vector manipulations and need calculus refreshers, and so on. Online instructors should anticipate these problem areas in their course design and then communicate about these difficult concepts and provide students with specific guidelines, tutorials, graphics, and references to help them grasp tricky concepts.

Communication is a two-way street. Online instructors also need to *listen* to what their students are saying through their questions and comments on discussion boards, in exams, and in lab reports. It is important to quickly recognize and correct any misperceptions before they are perpetuated. Written words have a substantial impact and should be as gentle as possible while still making a point—but not pointing a finger. Obviously, an instructor should never single out a student for criticism on a discussion board. It is much better to frame a correction by saying "There appears to be a misperception about XYZ" instead of "Joe is completely wrong about XYZ." However, students should definitely be identified and praised for good work: "Wow! Joe did a great job defining the steps he took on XYZ." This not only instills pride in Joe, it subconsciously makes Joe and other students want to do good work that will be acknowledged by their instructor. Interaction in an online class is vital so that students do not feel isolated (Maeroff, 2003).

Specific Tools and Software for Teaching Online Science

Computer technology, tools, and application knowledge is needed by all educators, but especially by those who teach online. This chapter reviews online tools and software used by experienced online science instructors as part of best practices for delivery of their courses. It includes examples provided by online lab science instructors to illustrate how they use computer tools. Many concepts and applications are obviously more complex than presented here, but mastering them is not beyond the capabilities of a dedicated science instructor.

The world of technology is rapidly evolving. Although specific applications are showcased in this chapter, there will no doubt be new versions, different platforms, and other technological changes by the time this book is read. Thus, the objectives of this chapter do not include instruction in the use of specific technologies, but rather are intended to describe types of software available to assist online science instructors; to indicate how this software functions and is used in online courses; and to show how software can facilitate communication with students and colleagues as well as aid in research projects. The following brief introductions to different online technologies should help science educators identify tools that could work well with their course objectives, content, delivery preferences, lab requirements, and students. This chapter provides only brief introductions to potentially useful online technology applications; more in-depth information can be obtained from the tutorials on the software's websites.

LEARNING MANAGEMENT SYSTEMS

The first and most important technology a science educator normally encounters in online education is a learning management system (LMS), also referred to as a course management system (CMS), or a virtual learning environment (VLE). Regardless of the name, these education-specific software application programs are typically licensed on an institution-wide basis for installation across all related campuses and departments, and they are utilized in support of campus-based course enrichment as well as online course delivery.

There are many learning management systems on the market. Although each may have unique features, they generally perform the same specific functions. LMS platforms allow educators to upload and deliver contact and scheduling information, course syllabi and lecture notes, plus content materials and multimedia elements. They also allow instructors to create, deliver, collect, and grade a variety of assessments and to communicate with students using e-mail, bulletin boards, discussion groups, blogs, and similar social networking tools. Students use an LMS to access their course content and assessments, to deliver their assignments, and to communicate with their instructor and classmates. The most widely used LMS platforms are the following:

Blackboard (www.blackboard.com), which recently acquired WebCT and Angel Learning and is used by over 70% of institutions (Green, 2009)

Desire2Learn (www.desire2learn.com)

Pearson LearningStudio (www.pearsoncustom.com/pearson-learning-studio), which was formerly eCollege

Moodle (www.moodle.com), a free, open-source LMS

Although not actually an LMS, *Wimba* (www.wimba.com) is collaboration software that offers comparable and compatible services that can either accompany or substitute for an LMS. The past several years have seen LMS developers merge into just a few companies. However, the lucrative LMS market associated with growing online enrollments continuously spawns new entrants into this field and spurs continuous improvement by established providers.

Some specialized curriculum-development tools allow online instructors to customize their course content without having to know HTML programming. Science educators can use these tools in a variety of ways to create and deliver content, promote interactions and communications, foster research and creativity, and evaluate academic integrity. They include the following:

SoftChalk LessonBuilder (www.softchalk.com)

Adobe eLearning Suite (www.adobe.com/resources/elearning)

MediaSite (www.sonicfoundry.com/default.aspx)

OpenOffice.org (www.openoffice.org/index.html)

Web Assign (www.webassign.net)

VIDEO-CONFERENCING TOOLS

An online anatomy and physiology professor at California State University San Marcos requires students to purchase a home lab kit to perform experiments including dissections and a web camera to video their lab reports (Perkins-Johnston, 2010). She uses a combination of PowerPoint slides, video, and the webcasting service *MediaSite* (http://www.sonicfoundry.com/mediasite) to present and broadcast her video-based syllabus and online course introduction to students. She appears on video on the left side of the screen and guides students through details of the PowerPoint slides that appear on the right side of the screen. This approach provides video, audio, text, and graphics simultaneously. In her presentation, she gives students

- her contact information and online office hours
- instructions for creating a video introduction of themselves
- a summary of chapter highlights
- examples of types of online assessments she will use
- details related to the lab kits students must use to perform lab assignments at home

Students are required to read and learn their course materials and to complete the lab activities detailed in the lab manual from their lab kit. They must use their video camera to produce and submit a video summary of their lab activities, which provides the instructor with assurance that they have done their lab work and are learning the material. Students report that they enjoy these video projects and feel the process of making the videos helps them to better learn the course materials. They often use other tools to enhance their presentations with music and multimedia elements, and they post their productions on *YouTube* (http://www.youtube.com) to share them beyond the classroom. By viewing the student video introductions, video lab reports, and required postings on the class discussion boards, the professor gets to know each online student and can gauge his or her level of understanding. She becomes familiar with each student's work and provides guidance as necessary. She is also aware if students' communications or the quality of their work drops off; if it does, she contacts them by e-mail, video conferencing, or phone.

Science instructors from other disciplines have also found success in having their students submit photo and video records of their lab work. For example, online geology instructors often have their students take self-guided field trips and include supporting photo and video records of their observations in their trip reports. Online students also use video recordings to illustrate problems they encounter so that their instructor can see their difficulty and better help them.

Web-conferencing tools are used in a variety of ways to facilitate online science classes and are particularly helpful in assisting visual learners and students new to lab work. Web-conferencing tools include webinars and chat rooms, which allow synchronistic visual and auditory communication between two or more people and offer the potential to be rebroadcast. Podcasting and videocasting or vodcasting may be used to record synchronous sessions, or an instructor may use them to produce supplemental course content. A web camera, microphone, and possibly a headset are required for web conferencing. Some conferencing tools are in the form of software that is downloaded into a computer, and others are web-based and accessed via a browser. Tool selection may be based on the system's requirements to record sessions for later viewing or to make the web conference public. The programs can include features such as file transfer, screen sharing, whiteboarding, and text-chat among participants. The primary consideration when selecting a conferencing tool is the number of participants expected to use it simultaneously. Most web-conferencing providers offer a free basic version but charge for upgraded features and large numbers of users.

Lab science instructors use video conferencing, podcasting, and vodcasting to demonstrate and explain lab experiment materials, processes, equipment, techniques, and other things that present challenges to students.

- Biology instructors find this approach useful in explaining the tools in the dissection kit and appropriate dissection techniques.
- Chemistry instructors explain safety measures related to handling of chemicals, dealing with flames and fumes, and performing certain testing procedures.
- Physics instructors use web-conferencing tools to explain experimental setups and illustrate complex calculations.

Free and popular one-to-one conference tools that allow instructors and students to see each other include the following:

Skype (www.skype.com) for up to 25 participants

Yahoo! Messenger (http://messenger.yahoo.com)

Windows Live (http://messenger.live.com)

Google Video Chat (http://mail.google.com/videochat)

Some science educators prefer multiparty video-conferencing tools so that several students can interact simultaneously to present their questions and share responses. Typically, the free services limit the number of participants. Fee-based tools not only allow more participants, but they also offer additional features including better video quality and some advanced customization capabilities. As with all technology, details are subject to change. The most popular fee-based multi-user web-conferencing software includes *WebEx* (http://www.webex.com), *Elluminate* (http://www.elluminate.com), and *Adobe ConnectNow* (http://www.adobe.com/acom/connectnow). However, there are also several excellent free multi-user web-conferencing tools, including these:

- *DimDim* (www.dimdim.com/products/dimdim-virtual-classroom.html) is a free program usable by up to 20 people on one operating system. Attendees can see the presenter's live video and desktop while hearing multiple voices over VoIP. Users can share PowerPoint presentations, PDF files, web pages, whiteboards, and desktops; attendees, if permitted by the host, can simultaneously annotate presentations, mark up whiteboards, send instant messages, and broadcast their audio and video. DimDim is targeting the education market and encouraging educators to create virtual classrooms with its product.

- *MeBeam* (www.mebeam.com) is a free web-based video-conferencing tool that allows up to 16 users but does not include the ability to record a session for viewing later.

- *FlashMeeting* (http://flashmeeting.e2bn.net) is a free web-based video-conferencing tool that allows multiparty video meetings with an unlimited number of people, but requires all users to have Adobe Flash installed on their computers.

WIKIS

Some educators encourage use of the information, collaboration, and research tools called wikis. *PBWorks for Classrooms* (http://pbworks.com/academic.wiki) was specifically produced for the education market. The basic edition is available at no charge for instructional use. It enables users to create public and private wiki workspace for educators and students to communicate and collaborate on documents, projects, lab work, and other types of work products. Key features include plug-ins for embedded video and audio; tags, RSS, and full-page revisions; plus student accountability that identifies who is making changes and automatically reverses those that are not authorized. More advanced features are fee-based.

Wikipedia (www.wikipedia.org) is the most widely used web-based general reference site today. It is a collaborative wiki written by volunteers from around the world and is promoted as a "free encyclopedia that anyone can edit." In reality, the site is well monitored, and the limitations on contributions are more stringent than implied. Although the reliability of Wikipedia information has dramatically improved, science instructors should still remind students that some of its content can be of questionable accuracy and encourage them to always verify Wikipedia by additional research. Instructors should also alert students to never copy text from Wikipedia pages in their lab reports and course assessments.

Diigo (www.diigo.com) explains its site as a research and collaborative research tool coupled with a knowledge-sharing community and social content. It allows users to bookmark pages relevant to their work or interests plus highlight sections of a web page and add sticky notes with personal comments. These annotations remain on the web pages when the user signs in and returns. Science instructors often recommend this tool because it allows students to consolidate their research, thoughts, and findings for group research projects.

ACADEMIC INTEGRITY TOOLS

Specialized software programs that deal with cheating, plagiarism, and other issues include these:

- *Viper*, a free download available at www.scanmyessay.com and other sites, is an anti-plagiarism scanner that became popular among on-campus and online educators and students via word of mouth and presentations at education conferences. Science educators can use this software to find out if students have copied content from the Internet, from other students, or even from their own prior lab reports and assignments. Students use Viper to confirm that they have not inadvertently omitted citations or inappropriately reused their own work. Many science educators keep a Viper database of each semester's lab reports and assignments to ensure that students are not submitting work done by others who have taken the course before them. To further strengthen the verification process, institutions are beginning to create databases of student work submitted to all its instructors for all class sections.

- *Turn It In* (www.turnitin.com) is another popular anti-plagiarism tool, produced by the education technology company iParadigms. It is usually licensed by institutions and directly integrated into their LMS.

SOCIAL-NETWORKING TOOLS

Social networking has become a popular way for educators to communicate with their students. Here are some of the more popular sites:

- *Facebook* (www.facebook.com) was originally used by college students but has expanded to include people of all ages who use it to connect with friends and family. Online professors use Facebook to get to know and communicate with their students, and students use it to better know classmates, communicate with those in their group projects, and share details about project experiences. However, anecdotal information indicates many students resent educators reaching out to them via Facebook, because they consider it to be their personal space for social interaction.

- *Twitter* (www.twitter.com) is becoming more popular in education as students and instructors post tweets, messages of 140 characters or less. They consider it a useful tool to communicate about assignments, course changes, and new resources to investigate.

- *MySpace* (www.myspace.com) is similar to Facebook with respect to primary users and content, but it is less frequently used in higher education.

- *LinkedIn* (www.linkedin.com) is geared toward business professionals who network for career and business opportunities. Many educators have LinkedIn profiles and are members of professional LinkedIn groups of interest to them, such as the National Science Foundation, National Science Teachers Association, eLearning Network, Online Educator, and the Sloan Consortium. Group members can post articles, pose questions for discussion, post job opportunities, and communicate about other activities appropriate for professional interactions.

- *Second Life* (www.secondlife.com) is a creativity tool that has received traction in education. Users create avatars to graphically represent themselves, and they interact alone or with others in the three-dimensional communities they create. In contrast to other creativity tools, users must download the free Second Life software into their computers. Discussions and demonstrations of this tool are popular topics at e-learning conferences as educators appear increasingly fascinated with its possibilities for engaging students in virtual learning and training.

SCIENCE-SPECIFIC TOOLS

Science educators tend to seek out effective web tools—especially shareware, freeware, open-source, and low-cost software—to share with their students and colleagues. The following are a few examples of specific software used in science education. Readers will find additional science-specific software referenced throughout this book, the names of which are bolded in the text when recommended or discussed by practicing online instructors. Similar and discipline-specific software is usually just an online search or collegial conversation away.

- *MathType* (www.dessci.com/en/products/mathtype) is an interactive equation editor for creating mathematical notation. It can be used with word processing programs, web pages, desktop publishing, PowerPoint presentations, and for TeX, LaTeX, and MathML documents. Science educators, especially those in chemistry and physics, usually find MathType very useful and easy to use. It works on both Windows and Mac operating systems and is compatible with hundreds of software applications.

- *Inkscape* (www.inkscape.org) is an open-source vector-graphics editor with capabilities similar to Illustrator, Freehand, CorelDraw, or Xara X. It uses the W3C standard Scalable Vector Graphics (SVG) file format and supports features including shapes, paths, text, markers, clones, alpha blending, transforms, gradients, patterns, and grouping as well as Creative Commons meta-data, node editing, layers, complex path operations, and bitmap tracing. Inkscape imports JPEG, PNG, TIFF, and other files and exports PNG and multiple vector-based formats. It is intended to be a powerful and convenient drawing tool compliant with XML, SVG, and CSS standards.

- *Fleye* (www.desktopgraphingcalculator.com) is a free desktop graphing calculator. It makes life easier for science students and educators by creating mathematical graphs for presentations in physics, differential equations, calculus, and the like. It graphs in eight different coordinate systems. Graphs and beautifully drawn functions can be saved as PNG and GIF files.

- *Jmol* (www.jmol.sourceforge.net) is a free open-source molecule viewer for students, educators, and researchers in chemistry and biochemistry. This applet is a stand-alone Java application that operates on the desktop and can be used to run an instructor's molecular library. It is a cross-platform that is compatible with Windows, Mac OS X, and Linux/Unix systems.

- *RasTop* (www.geneinfinity.org/rastop) is molecular visualization software. It is adapted from the program *RasMol* (http://rasmol.org), which is a molecular visualization freeware for proteins, DNA, and macromolecules. The software allows several molecules to be opened in the same window and several windows to be opened at the same time; users can manipulate numerous molecules to learn about them. In addition, users can export to the multi-platform ray-tracing package *POV-Ray* (www.povray.org) to create artistic renderings of molecules.

- *ACD Chemsketch* (www.acdlabs.com/resources/freeware/chemsketch/) freeware is an all-purpose chemical drawing and graphics program that can be used with templates or freehand. It allows students and instructors to draw a variety of chemical structures and to view them in 2D or 3D. Features include click-and-draw molecules, ions, stereo bonds, text, polygons, arrows, and lab apparatus icons. It can perform automatic calculation of molecular weights and formula weights. The developer, *ACDLabs* (www.acdlabs.com), also offers free downloads of several other utilities and template packages that extend the usefulness of ChemSketch.

- *KnowItAll* (www.knowitall.com/academic) is a free and fully functional software package that promotes students' learning and faculty research. This suite of programs is useful for drawing chemical structures, generating lab reports, interpreting spectra, analyzing molecular symmetry, and making general laboratory calculations. This set of tools is contained within a common interface, making it easy to learn and transfer data from application to application. The program includes free training movies to teach professors and students to get the most out of the software.

- *Orbital Viewer* (www.orbitals.com/orb/ov.htm) is an orbital drawing program with numerous features that comes in both Windows and command-line interface versions. It allows instructors and students to draw any atom or molecule, create animations, do cutaways, show the locations where probability goes to zero, light the orbital from any location, and cast shadows. It saves files in TIFF, PPM, BMP, AVI, and VRML formats.

- *Chemical Thesaurus* (www.chemthes.com) software uses a relational database to store information about any chemical reaction process, including radiochemistry, phase change, resonance structure interconversion, and interchanging conformation. The application software is extensively hyperlinked, making it very easy to explore. There are both a web-based version and a downloadable version.

Online Science Lab Options

Pros, Cons, and Effectiveness

Learning science is an active process. Learning science is something that students do, not something that is done to them. In learning science students describe objects and events, ask questions, acquire knowledge, construct explanations of natural phenomena, test those explanations in many different ways, and communicate their ideas to others.

National Science Education Standards (CSMEE, 1996, p. 20)

It has been well established that most science educators believe hands-on laboratory experimentation provides students with the best way to learn science and should be a component of lab science curriculums. This requirement is easy enough to satisfy if the course is conducted on a campus with formal laboratory facilities, but it poses problems if the related course is not conducted on campus. Over the years, educators have tried, with varying degrees of success, numerous methods and techniques to provide off-campus students with valid laboratory experiences.

THE OBJECTIVES OF SCIENCE LABORATORY EXPERIENCES

Before we examine various laboratory options, the essential functions of laboratory experimentation need to be reviewed. Educational institutions have long compiled lists of the rationales and objectives for the laboratory components that accompany science courses (Rice University, 2006). These traditionally include the following:

Students learn by doing.

Experimentation must teach basic laboratory techniques.

Experimentation must demonstrate and reinforce understanding of the scientific method.

Experimentation must teach the ability to adhere to instructions on laboratory safety, to recognize hazardous situations, and to act appropriately.

Students must learn to measure, manipulate, observe, and reason.

Students must develop scientific manipulative skills and perform quantitative experiments.

Experimentation should help students learn to manipulate and interpret numerical data.

Students must learn to observe, recognize, and interpret patterns in laboratory activities.

Students must develop the ability to keep careful records of experimental observations and to communicate with others about these observations and the conclusions drawn from them.

Experimentation should teach the ability to work independently and to also work effectively as part of a team.

Experimentation should show the relationship between measurement and scientific theory.

TRADITIONAL CAMPUS LABS

In higher education, science courses have traditionally been conducted on college campuses and have consisted of a live classroom-lecture component combined with an additional wet-lab component, usually performed at a separate time and in the campus's science laboratory facilities. This approach is referred

Learning Objectives for Undergraduate Natural Science Laboratory Experiences

Acquire basic laboratory skills

- Learn to observe, measure, record, convert, and analyze data.
- Learn lab safety, recognize potential hazards, and act appropriately.

Acquire communication and recording skills

- Learn to keep timely, comprehensive lab notes for work replication.
- Clearly and concisely communicate research data and experimental results.
- Improve oral and written communication and presentation skills.

Gain maturity and responsibility

- Learn advanced preparation and organization skills plus the value of mistakes.
- Work independently and as a part of a team.

Understand the context of science

- Recognize the relevance of accurate data gathering and measurement.
- Learn and appreciate the processes and concepts of the scientific method.
- Relate lab results and experiences to the real world.
- Appreciate the major consequences of minor oversights.

Integrate knowledge and experience

- Appreciate and apply critical thinking skills in science and other work.
- Apply math, science, and logical processes to science and other work.
- Skeptically evaluate cause-and-effect conclusions in science and society.
- Recognize when arguments and positions do and do not make sense.

Summarized from Rice University laboratory educators in natural sciences and engineering

to as face-to-face (F2F) learning. A fully equipped and stocked campus laboratory is assumed to provide online students with ideal opportunities to experience science in all the ways envisioned by the above rationales and objectives.

In the laboratory, undergraduate students are normally placed into groups ranging from two to four and occasionally up to six or more students. They are provided with science materials such as chemicals, specimens, microscopes, measuring and analysis equipment, personal safety items, and any other tools required to perform an assigned scientific experiment. Although these laboratories usually contain sophisticated electronic equipment, undergraduate students rarely have the opportunity to operate that equipment and usually are only told how it works or allowed to observe it being used by an instructor or aide.

The groups of students use a lab manual and are allocated a set amount of time to review an experiment's objectives, conduct the activity, observe and document results, and then analyze the data, formulate conclusions, and prepare notes for a formal lab report. By going through this hands-on, tactile process of employing the scientific method, it is expected that students will learn and understand the science concepts covered in their course and develop good critical thinking and problem-solving skills. In academic circles this traditional science laboratory experience is considered to be the gold standard of science learning.

However, science instructors are increasingly acknowledging the reality that not all students are benefiting from their traditional science laboratory experiences. This unfortunate situation is usually attributed to institutional limitations, not the facilities or instructors. Many institutions suffer from a lack of adequate science laboratory space, resources, and personnel to provide ideal laboratory experiences for undergraduate students. They primarily compensate by arranging science students into lab groups of a sufficient size to be "processed" as efficiently as possible within the space and time available. Usually one student in the group takes the lead and actually performs the experiment and manipulates the science materials. Another student may be the record keeper, but most students have little opportunity to handle the materials or perform any meaningful lab work. Typically, remaining group members engage in private conversations while feigning interest in the laboratory activities in which they cannot participate and thus are only superficially engaged.

Most educators believe campus-based laboratory experiences are effective tools for teaching science, and indeed they are, under ideal circumstances that allow each student to actively perform all experiments and utilize the full spectrum of laboratory equipment. Unfortunately, ideal circumstances are not the reality in the majority of today's over-crowded, underfunded, and understaffed campus laboratories. Even if laboratories contain highly sophisticated laboratory equipment, rarely are undergraduate students allowed to operate it. This reality is forcing instructors to question the true value of traditional campus-based laboratory experiences for the average undergraduate student.

SIMULATIONS AND VIRTUAL LABS

Science simulations usually take the form of computer-based, graphic virtual representations and interactive enactments of laboratory experiments or exercises. Professional simulations play relevant and important reinforcing and training roles in education and industry. For example, the military and NASA train pilots in sophisticated simulators before allowing them to fly real fighter jets and space shuttles. Before cutting into a cadaver, much less an actual patient, Harvard medical students explore all the layers and organs of the human body in minute detail via cutting-edge simulations created from painstakingly compiled images of micromillimeter slices of cadavers. Professionals training for advanced careers in disaster preparedness and management interact with a variety of simulated scenarios that put them and their staffs through their paces before they are faced with real-world catastrophes.

High-level computer simulations can undoubtedly play a vital complementary role in educational experiences and help students better learn processes and understand complex principles and relationships from the safety of a virtual environment. Unfortunately, simulations of such extraordinary sophistication that genuinely reflect reality cost hundreds of millions of dollars to develop. Where they do exist, such computer simulations are rarely available to undergraduate science students. This situation is unlikely to change until higher education and community colleges have access to the type of economic resources available to NASA, the military, and private industry.

In the early years of online education, as a response to limited laboratory facilities, science instructors hoped that computer simulations would be the panacea to provide students with a valid substitute for laboratory experiences. As computer technology has become more sophisticated, laboratory simulations have continuously improved and are successfully utilized to complement numerous science course curriculums. These virtual labs include multimedia elements, high-resolution visuals, audio instructions, interactive tutorials, and other elements to enhance learning and retention. Table 4.1 delineates pros and cons of computer simulations.

Undoubtedly, simulations can play a useful complementary role in certain types of educational experiences. Different types of high-level simulations allow students to interface and essentially interact with relevant learning materials in a safe virtual environment. Health fields, engineering, environmental and physical

Table 4.1.
Computer Simulations as Substitutes
for Traditional Lab Experiences

Pros	Cons
Students like them because they are easy and like computer games.	They meet few lab learning objectives.
They can be found online and are relatively cheap or free.	They are inadequate for major-level work.
They meet some lab learning objectives.	Students miss tactile experiences.
They are useful as pre-labs and for reinforcing important concepts.	They are too passive for deep learning.
There are no liability issues or facilities costs.	They may not be adequately challenging.
	Professional science organizations consider them inadequate lab substitutes.
	Students are seeing science instead of doing science.
	They may not be accepted for transferable course credits.
	Good ones are very expensive to create.

sciences, computer sciences, and numerous other important fields of study frequently use high-tech simulations to explain processes, complex principles, and relationships. Many respected colleges and universities including MIT, Stanford University, and Brigham Young University have developed and employ virtual laboratory simulations. However, these institutions utilize their excellent simulations as pre-labs or a supplements to the content of their courses rather than a substitute for real-world, hands-on laboratory experiences, which they separately provide their students.

Despite their valid roles in supporting and reinforcing science education, simulated computer laboratory experiences continue to be judged by educators and major science education organizations as ineffective substitutes for traditional, tactile laboratory experiences. The National Science Teachers Association (2009) states, "For science to be taught properly and effectively, [wet] labs must be an integral part of the science curriculum." In light of decades of declining science literacy and the evidence that laboratory experimentation is vital to understanding science and the science learning process, students undoubtedly need greater exposure to lab science courses that provide genuine hands-on lab experiences. The American Chemical Society (2009) has taken an unequivocal position that simulations are not a valid substitute for tactile labs. These influential voices have combined to insist that national education standards require tactile, wet-lab experiences for accredited and transferable credits.

Simulations are occasionally quite useful, especially in replacing extremely dangerous or hazardous experiments. Yet, simulations cannot begin to replace true laboratory experience because they are ill-suited for delivering a realistic environment to conduct experiments, to measure results, to determine error, and to appreciate lab safety considerations. Simulations tend to be basically passive like computer games; to not fully engage students in relating science to themselves and the real world; to restrict students to a narrow investigative path; and to offer no opportunity to explore their errors or the implications of them. Most simulations are physically unconvincing and never provide the ambiguous results that normally occur with real instruments and promote critical questioning of cause-and-effect evaluations. For these reasons, increasing numbers of institutions are refusing to accept transferred science credits if a course's laboratory component was performed solely or primarily via computer simulations.

REMOTE ACCESS LABS

Modern remote access technology allows scientists to schedule time on the Hubble Telescope and to fully operate it from nearly anywhere in the world at almost any time of their choosing. Similarly an Air Force pilot based in New Mexico can remotely operate a drone airplane flying across the mountains of Afghanistan and instruct it take photos and drop bombs as it flies across hostile locations that are too dangerous for human pilots. Renowned cardiovascular surgeons in New York City can remotely access a surgical robot in France and actually use it to perform heart surgery on patients who are thousands of miles away.

This same type of technology allows remote access to some of the world's most technologically advanced science laboratory instrumentation.

Academic remote access labs (RALs) are often lumped into the computer simulation category because RALs are accessed via science students' computers. However, unlike simulations that try to replicate real-world experiences, RALs actually are real-world experiences because they provide access to fully functioning advanced scientific instrumentation that is actually used daily in genuine, real-world science applications and investigations.

RALs allow students working from a home or campus computer to conduct genuine experimentation on remote laboratory instruments. Students can thus analyze data via highly sophisticated instrumentation that in the past was available only to high-level professionals. Because RALs can be accessed 24/7, students have the opportunity to utilize this state-of-the-art technology at almost any time and from almost anywhere. These possibilities are leading to the development of new teaching strategies and exciting new collaborative opportunities for undergraduate science students.

Today a student can perform an experiment using a commercially produced lab kit to manually perform an experiment and gain a basic understanding of the conceptual components of a particular scientific process. The student can then use additional lab kit materials to acquire and prepare sample materials that are sent to the Integrated Laboratory Network (ILN), a remote laboratory facility sponsored by Western Washington State University. The ILN houses extremely complex scientific instrumentation that is beyond the economic capabilities of most institutions to acquire.

At a prescheduled time, an ILN technician and the student interact via computer. The technician inputs the student's samples into various sophisticated instrumentation including a mass spectrometer, a flame atomic absorption unit, and a gas chromatograph. The student receives instructions and is allowed to operate this equipment from his or her computer, fully test the previously prepared samples, and immediately receive a complete report on the test results, which can then be compared to the tactile experiment previously performed. This is a genuine real-world experience because the instrumentation used by the student is the same instrumentation that is used by research scientists, crime lab investigators, and technical medical specialists.

Remote access can add rich and genuine science laboratory experiences for students who lack access to such advanced scientific instrumentation in their own communities. The increasing availability of this type of access is already

Table 4.2.
Remote Access Labs as Substitutes for
Traditional Lab Sessions

Pros	Cons
Enrich and reinforce tactile labs	Are not yet readily available
Provide real-world technology experience	Require pre-planning and scheduling
Perform advanced and dangerous labs	Can be costly
Meet most lab learning objectives	Do not meet all lab learning objectives

changing some of the methodology for teaching instrument-based science. Table 4.2 sums up the pros and cons of remote access labs.

HYBRID LABS

When a science course is listed as a hybrid, that usually implies the lecture and content portions of the course are taught online, but students are required to attend scheduled laboratory sessions on campus. Hybrid courses are offered by institutions and instructors who believe students must have hands-on laboratory experiences and that the only way to effectively provide them is to bring students to the campus's formal laboratory facilities.

Hybrid labs certainly fulfill the vital and traditional wet-lab objectives and experiences required for science learning and allow students to acquire fully accredited and transferable lab science credits. Because students taking hybrid science courses often live at a considerable distance from the campus and/or are also working adults, the hybrid lab sessions are usually offered via full-day session over several weekends during the semester.

There are two basic drawbacks to this form of hybrid lab science course. The first deals with the timing of the labs. Normally labs are spread out through a term, and the experiments to be performed each week correspond to the learning objectives then being studied. Because hybrid labs are usually held less frequently and in all-day sessions, there is the potential for a substantial disconnect between the lab experiences and the course content materials being studied at that time. Also, students often become fatigued by marathon lab sessions and their learning tends to be impaired as they strive to complete day-long and possibly mind-numbing sessions of back-to-back science experiments.

The second drawback of hybrid labs is that they require students to come to campus, which for most students completely defeats their purpose in taking an online course. Students usually take online courses to specifically achieve needed flexibility in scheduling their studies around work, family, and other commitments. If they are unable to achieve that goal with one institution's online lab science courses, there is a high probability that they will take those lab science courses from a different institution that offers them fully online. Plus, they may then decide to take their other courses from that institution too. Table 4.3 summarizes the advantages and disadvantages of hybrid labs.

Table 4.3.
Hybrid Lab Sessions as Substitutes for Traditional Lab Sessions

Pros	Cons
Exactly replicate traditional labs	Require students to come to campus
Provide hands-on science activities	Defeat the objectives of online courses
Provide access to formal lab materials	Limit course's enrollment to students within commuting distance
Fulfill all laboratory learning objectives	Increase institution's facilities expenses for personnel, insurance, and materials costs
Provide transferable course credits	When conducted in a few intensive full-day or weekend sessions during the term
	• experiments may not be performed when the concepts are being taught in the course
	• the focus may be on the completion of experiments in lieu of relating outcomes to concepts
	• student fatigue often negates learning

The files of Hands-On Labs contain histories of a few small institutions that tried offering their hybrid lab students the option of commercial science lab kits instead of coming to campus to perform labs. This option provided a convenience to students who could not attend scheduled lab sessions. It also gave the instructors an opportunity to compare outcomes between the different lab options. Rather than attending campus sessions, students soon overwhelmingly selected the commercial lab kits, even though they had to purchase them separately. Because the learning outcomes were actually a bit better for the lab-kit students, within a few semesters those institutions dropped their hybrid lab sessions and now offer their courses fully online with lab kits to satisfy their course laboratory components.

KITCHEN SCIENCE LABS

Science experimentation using common elements found in a typical home kitchen can provide excellent learning experiences for elementary and middle school students. However, this method is not usually considered adequate or appropriate for higher education and rarely for college-level science majors' lab courses. Despite its genuine basis in science, college students tend to not respect kitchen chemistry and to feel it is too simple for the higher levels of learning they expect. Science educators are inclined to share this view and believe higher education courses for both science majors and nonscience majors should have a traditional laboratory learning component. This is especially important for science majors and community college or career college students who expect to transfer to a four-year program and need to ensure their lab science course credits will be accepted.

Despite these criticisms, a few exceptional kitchen chemistry lab courses have been developed for introductory college chemistry. Most notable of these is the "anytime anywhere chemistry experience" developed in 2001–2002 under a Fund for the Improvement of Secondary Education (FIPSE) grant by associate professors of chemistry Jimmy Reeves of the University of North Carolina at Wilmington and Doris Kimbrough of the University of Colorado at Denver. Analysis of comparative results found that students performing these kitchen labs at home outscored their campus peers on their lab practicum by about 10 points. This project received a Sloan-C Award for Effective Practices in 2003 and showed that students will diligently work to perform laboratory experiments at home and that kitchen chemistry experiments can enhance students' appreciation for how chemistry is relevant to their daily lives.

Lyall and Patti (2010) agree that kitchen chemistry may provide a suitable approach in introductory chemistry courses and for students who require only a basic knowledge of chemistry. However, they feel kitchen chemistry experiments are not adequate for students who intend to make a career in chemistry, biochemistry, or other disciplines that require a high degree of chemical experimentation.

On the downside, implementing kitchen chemistry experiments often requires the student to construct simple science equipment so it's easy for the science lessons to get lost in equipment-construction logistics. Another challenge with kitchen labs is that the results can vary significantly, depending on the brand of materials used. The chemical composition and purity in the typical household cleaners used in kitchen labs can vary substantially by brand names.

Kitchen labs can also be quite expensive and wasteful when they require the purchase of products students do not normally have in their homes, apartments, or dorms. A kitchen lab can require a substantial amount of time as well as money if students have to shop at several stores to find all the items needed to perform an experiment. In addition, a student may need only a small amount of a substance, such as a few grams of Borax, but can purchase it in nothing smaller than a five-pound box for $11. If an experiment requires several such items, the kitchen lab approach can be time consuming as well as very expensive and wasteful. An internal HOL study comparing household items that could approximate the chemicals in a lab kit's ionic reaction experiment found that even if the smallest available quantities of the household items were bought to replicate each chemical, the student would pay at least four times the cost of the lab kit's experiment bag. Thus, instructors who believe kitchen chemistry labs will save their students money are possibly mistaken.

Another presumed advantage of kitchen science labs is that students can easily find the required experimentation materials at home, but this too is seldom the case. As previously discussed, required materials can be very expensive and time consuming to find, and often students simply do not want to be bothered. Table 4.4 summarizes the plusses and minuses of kitchen labs.

Like many instructors who care more about students' finances than the students do, Dr. Peter Jeschofnig tried the kitchen lab approach for a few semesters of his calculus-based online physics course. He prepared a list with detailed specifications for each item the students would need to acquire to perform their experiments and even included the names of several shops and online links where the items could be bought. A few students diligently acquired all materials and had no problems performing the labs. But the majority of students seemed to have at least a few procurement problems during the semester and continually complained about the hassles with obtaining their materials. Many students procrastinated in filling their supply list and were then late with assignments because some item was not available or was on backorder at Radio Shack. Dr. Jeschofnig experienced no further complaints after switching to a commercially assembled physics lab kit in 2003. Even though students could purchase the kit's individual materials at a fraction of the commercial kit's cost, having all needed items handily packaged together apparently has greater value to them than saving money.

Table 4.4.
Kitchen Labs as Substitutes for
Traditional Lab Sessions

Pros	Cons
Provide hands-on science activities	Limited sophistication of experiments
Relate science to the real world	Illustrate primarily basic concepts
Can fulfill most laboratory learning objectives	Questionable adequacy for college-level work
Assumed to be cheap and easy	Students do not respect as serious science
May provide transferable course credits	Quality varies from creative to inadequate
No facilities-related expenses	Time and costs required to obtain materials and construct equipment
	Cost of acquiring materials can be substantial
	Lab results can vary by products used
	Potential safety and liability issues
	No learning advantages over campus labs

Despite their real-world connections, the bottom line is that kitchen science labs have no learning advantage over traditional laboratory experiences. Their supposed advantages in cost and convenience are a myth. The majority of higher education's science instructors believe kitchen science labs are overly simplistic and not suitable or acceptable substitutes for accredited college-level laboratory experiences.

INSTRUCTOR-ASSEMBLED LABS

Several very dedicated online science educators who apparently have a lot of spare time, or who have made time for the sake of their students, have designed lab kits around their course's lab manual and then assembled lab kit supplies for their students to either buy or check out. Most of these instructor-designed kits are very good and provide great home-based science learning experiences for their students.

Unfortunately, because these instructors are educators first and not business-people or stock clerks, the logistics of assembling lab kits soon becomes fatiguing and frustrating. These instructors must first determine all the different materials, chemicals, specimens, equipment, beakers, pipettes, and other equipment that the students will need to perform the experiments; these can total a hundred or more individual items. Then suppliers for each item must be located so that pricing, terms, and shipping can be negotiated. The instructors must also familiarize themselves with constantly changing government regulations and ensure that any chemicals and materials they intend to provide are in compliance. When the supplies arrive, they must be unpacked, sorted, allocated, and repackaged into the students' lab kits. Then the kits must be distributed to the students or through the bookstore, and then purchase or deposit details must be settled. Table 4.5 lists the pros and cons of instructor-assembled kits.

One online science professor in Alaska stocks several dozen science items in her office and requires her students to come to campus to check them out at the beginning of the semester and to return them at the end. These commutes can be an inconvenience for many students.

Instructors usually require students to return borrowed science equipment and supplies at the end of the term, then the instructor or a lab tech must verify each inventory item to ensure it can be reused by another student the following term. Anger and irritation plus settlement charges for costs related to missing and damaged items must be negotiated. Returned items must be inventoried

Table 4.5.
Instructor-Assembled Kits as Substitutes
for Traditional Lab Sessions

Pros	Cons
Provide hands-on science activities	Requires investment of time and multiple resources by instructor or institution, or both
Fulfill laboratory learning objectives	Safety concerns and liability issues
Assumed to be cheap and easy	Purchasing, stocking, assembly, packaging, accounting, and restocking issues
Provide transferable course credits	Instructor relegated to stock-clerk chores
	Inevitable disputes regarding returns
	Potential conflict of interest and distractions from teaching responsibilities

and counted so that replacement materials can be ordered and the process can begin again.

Within a few terms, most instructors who try this approach abandon it. After they begin to calculate the uncompensated time they and their lab assistants spend on this enterprise and to consider the hassles and headaches it creates, they soon decide their time would be better allocated to teaching and having meaningful interactions with students instead of worrying about lab kit supplies. These instructors also begin to recognize the potential liability risks of such an endeavor. Most of them finally conclude that although providing science lab kits to students is a good thing on one level, on another level it can be an exceptionally inefficient use of their professional time as an educator.

COMMERCIALLY ASSEMBLED LAB KITS

It is reasonable to expect that laboratory experiences that accompany online science courses should achieve levels of outcome similar to campus-based laboratory experiences. No lesser standards should be acceptable in considering substitute laboratory experiences for online science courses (Jeschofnig, 2009).

Thus, the same standards applied to on-campus labs must be applied to any commercially assembled lab kits that are used with online science courses.

Commercially designed and assembled lab kits for higher education tend to be sophisticated, academically aligned boxed collections of appropriate science materials. Such kits have been designed, produced, and distributed by Hands-On Labs (HOL; www.LabPaq.com) since 1994 and are available in all science disciplines for undergraduate college and high school students. These include introductory, science major, and non-major course kits for biology, human anatomy and physiology, microbiology, nutrition, chemistry, physics, physical sciences, geology and earth sciences, environmental sciences, and forensics. (Note: The authors of this book are the owners of HOL, which they founded specifically to produce the academically aligned science lab kits they have developed in conjunction with experienced online laboratory science educators.)

Other science kit suppliers include eScience Labs (http://esciencelabs.com), which has been producing a limited but increasing number of commercially assembled kits since 2008. These are primarily designed for the middle and high school markets, but they also produce some kits for college-level courses. Quality Science Labs (www.qualitysciencelabs.com) is a small, home-based company that also produces lab kits for the middle and high school markets. With the growth in online education and the evidence of effectiveness demonstrated by HOL over the past decade, it is reasonable to expect additional commercial lab kit suppliers to soon appear.

Commercially assembled science lab kits have the potential to address all the needs and issues thus far discussed regarding science laboratory experiences for online students. A well-designed and well-equipped lab kit that is academically aligned to specific course objectives will mirror the types of experiments that students normally perform in campus labs. The price of commercial lab kits can run into the hundreds of dollars, but they normally contain a related lab manual as well as needed science equipment and supplies. Kit costs are usually offset by convenience, commuting-related savings, and savings from not having to purchase a separate lab manual.

All the traditional requirements and objectives expected of a laboratory science learning experience can usually be met by commercially assembled lab kits. Students have valid interaction with science equipment and materials, engage in measurement and quantitative activities, experience learning from manipulation and observation, have the opportunity to make and mature from mistakes,

Table 4.6.
Commercially Assembled Lab Kits as Substitutes
for Traditional Lab Sessions

Pros	Cons
Replicate traditional wet campus labs	Additional cost for students
Aligned to match course content	May require adoption contracts by manufacturers for production purposes
Meet all laboratory learning objectives	No immediate instructor assistance or peer communications
Provide transferable course credits	More challenging and time consuming for students
Include lab manual and required materials	
Convenient and easy to use	
No time, place, or scheduling limitations	
Safe, fully insured, and shipped direct	

and integrate their math and language skills by computing and communicating experimental results. They also learn to logically and pragmatically approach problem solving as they physically perform steps of the scientific method and develop the critical thinking skills required for analysis of results from their scientific experimentation activities. Table 4.6 summarizes the strengths and weaknesses of commercially assembled kits.

Unlike computer simulations, commercial lab kits physically engage students in active learning. Unlike the marathon lab sessions of hybrid labs, commercial lab kits allow students to perform and learn from experiments in rhythm with the flow of course content. Unlike the simpleness of kitchen science labs, commercial lab kits provide students with genuine science equipment, chemicals, and specimens to work with. Unlike the inconvenience of student-supplied labs, commercial lab kits conveniently provide consistency in materials as well as the necessary science supplies, which can be stored in the kit box. Unlike instructor-assembled labs, commercial lab kits contain nothing that needs to be returned and are fully insured to protect the user, the user's institution, and the user's instructor.

We have worked in distance science education for over two decades and have personally tried and tested every conceivable substitute for traditional laboratory experiences available, including all of those previously discussed. None ever came close to the levels of convenience, personal satisfaction, and educational opportunities for both students and instructors that are provided by commercially assembled science lab kits. Other instructors may prefer other ways of providing substitute laboratory experiences. However, we and scores of online lab science instructors we know who have traveled similar paths find our students' learning experiences with commercially designed and assembled science lab kits are equivalent to or better than those of our F2F campus students. Further, we believe commercially assembled lab kits are the most practical and effective way to provide engaging and valid laboratory opportunities for online students while freeing instructors from laboratory management duties and providing more valuable time for interacting with students.

Evidence Supporting the Effectiveness of Commercial Science Lab Kits

Several comparisons have been made of F2F campus vs. online student assessments where the course content plus lab assignments and assessments were equivalent and the only difference was that F2F labs were conducted on campus and online labs were conducted with commercial lab kits.*

CCCOnline, Denver, CO, a survey of online student satisfaction asking students' lab preference (Vorndam, 2007).

- 25.2% of respondents preferred campus labs over home lab kits
- 9.9% were indifferent
- 64.8% of respondents exclusively preferred lab kits

Ocean County College, NJ, a comparison of Human Anatomy and Physiology Society national exam scores (Jeschofnig & Spencer, 2008).

- F2F range 26–74, mean of 45.09
- Online range 28–80, mean of 45.73

Herkimer County Community College (SUNY), NY, a comparison of students using the Science Major's Biology Kit (Herzog, 2008). Online students substantially outperformed F2F:

- 62% of online students scored an A or B (average grade = 87.5)
- 43% of F2F students scored an A or B (average grade = 75.8)

Colorado Mountain College, CO, first- and second-semester chemistry, a comparison of equivalent scores on pre- and post-course American Chemical Society proctored exams (Jeschofnig, 2009). Online students outperformed F2F students by 5% in lab grades and 1% in overall grades.

CCCOnline, Denver, CO (Lormand, K., biology professor, personal communication with L. Jeschofnig, November 4, 2009):

- Introductory College Biology: 93% of online students made a C or better during the spring 2008 semester versus 77% of F2F students.
- General Biology: Since the fall of 2004, online students have outscored F2F students by an average of 6.3% on their mean final exam scores. Spring 2008 mean final exam scores were 83% for online students and 72% for F2F students.
- Anatomy & Physiology I: Since the fall of 2004, online students have outscored F2F students by an average of 7.5% on their mean final exam scores. Spring 2008 mean final exam scores were 78% for online students and 71% for F2F students.

Hands-On Labs, Inc., survey of fall 2008 LabPaq users conducted via Constant Contact (HOL, 2009). Over 87% of responding online students using LabPaq kits achieved an A (65%) or B (22%) in their lab science course, and 80% were very satisfied with their experience.

---

*Comments and data are based upon the use of Hand-On Labs' LabPaq kits.

The Art of Teaching an Online Science Course

We hope the preceding chapters have convinced the reader that lab sciences should and can be taught online, and you are excited and eager to get started. This chapter provides relevant instructions and best practices for quickly establishing a dynamic online science course that is relevant, effective, and satisfying—to instructors as well as students.

START WITH A COMPREHENSIVE SYLLABUS

Online science instructors who are willing to invest initial time and energy in creating a pedagogically thorough syllabus will save themselves innumerable headaches throughout the semester. An online course syllabus needs to be very explicit and cover every aspect of the course. It should provide clear and complete explanations about how the course will be conducted and how student work will be assessed, and it should explicitly state what is expected of the students. It should be posted as soon as possible before the beginning of the semester so that students can determine if the course is right for them before enrolling or before the refund/census drop date and so that eager students can get a head start on their coursework if they want. The syllabus should remain posted throughout the semester so that students can refer to it when needed and it can be an arbitrator of disputes.

Essential Elements of a Good Lab Science Syllabus

Instructor information and accessibility

- *Instructor's name* and preferred title: "Thomas Smith, PhD, but please call me Dr. Tom."

- External as well as internal *e-mail addresses*. This is needed in case the LMS is down.

- *Phone numbers.* Include the time zone and appropriate times to call for each number: "By Appointment Only: Please e-mail me to set up a phone conference appointment" *or* "Call my cell between 1 p.m. and 5 p.m. MST, but call my home between 5 p.m. and 9 p.m. MST."

- *Online hours* are specific times within an identified time zone when the instructor agrees to always be available via e-mail, online chat, or for phone calls.

- *Online response times* are at the discretion of the instructor, but should be stated and followed so that students will know what to expect and will time their inquiries accordingly: "I normally check e-mail around noon and 8 p.m. on weekdays and again on Sunday evenings, but life happens, so this schedule is subject to change."

Tech support contact information

Include all names, phone numbers, time zones, e-mail addresses, and contact hours for the institution's technical and administrative support staff.

Course information

- Course title and course number

- *Course description:* This should match the description in the course catalog.

- *Credit hours:* In addition to the number of credits to be earned, this is a good place to describe the amount of work normally associated with those credits. This information is extremely important for time-intensive lab science courses where students need to schedule adequate time to perform their lab experiments: "This is a 5-credit course. To do well in this course, you should allocate at least 15 to 20 hours per week to your studies, and at least a third of that time should be dedicated to completing lab assignments.

- *Prerequisites:* Online lab sciences courses are very demanding and require self-discipline, time management, computer knowledge, plus excellent math and language skills. Science students without these skills should be identified early enough to seek remediation or to drop the course without penalty.

  - *Skill Assessments:* In addition to the institution's required prerequisites, it is wise to provide science students with links to online assessment instruments for math and writing skills and to ascertain if they are genuinely capable of handling the course requirements. Many science instructors find the distance learning assessment tool READI from eLearning Toolbox to be a valuable resource for this purpose. A product demonstration is available at www.readi.info/

- *Computer capabilities:* Students need access to a functional computer and an Internet connection—preferably high speed. They should also have appropriate software and be capable of navigating the Internet, performing online research, and using document, spreadsheet, and e-mail programs.

- *Expected competencies and outcomes:* These should match the ones listed in the institution's course catalog.

Course materials

- *Textbooks, software, simulation CDs, lab kits, and other required materials:* List the exact titles, ISBN numbers, and other identifying information for all required course materials. Although the exact prices of these items should not be quoted because they can change, give a general estimate for the total cost of all course materials so that students understand up front what kind of financial investment will be required.

  - State which materials are absolutely required and which are optional.

  - Include any special purchasing instructions such as product codes and online links to specialty providers.

  - Note for which items proof of purchase may be required so that students will know to keep their receipts: "This course requires you to use a commercially assembled lab kit to complete your laboratory assignments. Because these assignments cannot be fulfilled without the kit, you may be required to provide proof of your lab kit purchase, so save your receipt!"

- *Course equipment:* List equipment that will be needed, such as computer hardware requirements, digital camera, video camera, and programmable calculator.

Course activities and design

Briefly describe how the course will be conducted and what activities will be undertaken. "This 15-week online lab science course will be conducted within Blackboard and cover 14 weekly learning modules. The 15th week will be used for review and the final exam. Each module will consist of textbook and online reading assignments, research and discussion topics, and a laboratory assignment, each with a specific due date as identified in the course calendar. Assessments for a course grade will be based upon weekly quizzes (25%), lab reports and lab quizzes (25%), discussion-board participation (25%), and four major exams (25%). To begin, log into Blackboard and

(Continued)

click the Let's Get Started link for information on how to proceed and succeed in this course."

Course calendar

It is important to include a comprehensive course calendar that reflects every assignment's due date and even suggested start dates, especially for multi-step lab assignments. Online science students often report that a critical feature to their success in the course was a well-organized calendar that provided links to all lessons, assignments, laboratories, and quizzes (Carnevale, 2002).

- It should also include drop dates and any dates the instructor expects to be unavailable.

- The calendar should be as detailed as possible and give actual dates rather than merely show assignments by the week.

- It is helpful to color code the calendar for easy reference by associating different colors with different types of assignments such as red for exams, green for labs, blue for quizzes, and purple for readings.

- Students should be able to rely on the calendar, so it should not be changed during the semester unless absolutely necessary. Regardless, technology and other timing glitches happen, so warn students that the calendar is "subject to change at the discretion of the instructor should any scheduling allowances need to be made."

- Any calendar changes should be prominently announced on the log-in page and mentioned several times within discussion-board postings. To ensure that no student misses very important changes, it is wise to also send students direct e-mails.

Assignments

A list of assignments lets students know exactly what will be expected of them and allows them to work ahead if they desire and their instructor approves.

- State the time frame for completing the course and if assignments and lab reports are due on specific dates or if they may be self-paced within certain parameters.

- Identify which, if any, assignments will and will not be accepted early and state approximately when assignments will be graded and the grades posted. Typically, it is not a good idea to allow early postings to the discussion board. However, potential future discussion questions can be posted in advance so that students can contemplate them as they progress through the course materials

- In addition to due dates, each assignment should be clearly described. State how it is to be submitted—by e-mail or uploaded into the LMS. State also if handwritten and scanned or faxed assignments are acceptable. Except for math calculations, handwritten assignments should be discouraged because they are more difficult to read, store, and electronically grade. Besides, all students should be able to word-process their assignments, including math calculations.

- Define how e-mail subject lines and assignments should be titled: "Begin all e-mail subject lines and assignment titles with BIO-111, your last name, first name, and the date of submittal followed by the type and title of the assignment: BIO-111, Smith, Joe, 10/25/10 Lab Report: Scientific Method."

- Define how assignments should be formatted—such as "12point Arial font, double spaced" and what kind of files will be accepted, such as .doc, .xls, .rtf, .pdf.

- Define grades and grading policies; explain how assignments are graded and reveal any tools such as rubrics so that students will know exactly what is expected to make top grades. Show how and to what extent each assignment affects the final grade: "Labs—You will perform and write formal lab reports on 12 experiments. Labs reports represent 25% of the final grade, and each report is graded per the 100-point grading rubric shown in Appendix A."

- Consider advising students that course management software may track their online movements and record how much time they spend working within different sections of the learning management system. Even if you do not frequently check this data, knowing it is a possibility may be an additional motivator for students to do their work. However, some instructors prefer to not tell students about this LMS capability for fear students may try to foil the system and mislead the instructor about their work habits. These instructors prefer to keep LMS tracking capabilities as a secret weapon to detect if students are keeping up with the course.

- Advise students to save and back up all their assignments and lab reports to protect themselves in the event of a computer or system crash.

- List the assignments students will be required to complete:

  - *Required reading:* Also include dates when readings are expected to be completed for discussion and quiz purposes.

  - *Homework, special papers, and projects*

  - *Lab assignments:* Advise students to always read their lab assignments at least a week in advance, preferably upon completion of the previous lab assignment, in case there are any materials to be acquired or steps to be completed early. This also helps make more relevant the related materials that will be studied prior to performing the lab. It is also helpful for the instructor to warn students about experimental procedures that may take additional time, such as a culture or reaction that will have to be observed for several days.

  - *Discussion board participation:* Provide details about the expected quality and quantity of postings within set times for both the course and the lab discussion

(Continued)

boards. Students should know the minimum number of postings required and how many may be considered excessive. Give examples of good postings that add to the group's knowledge base and unacceptably brief postings such as "I agree."

- *Online quizzes and exams*: Advise whether quizzes and exams are open- or closed-book, if they are timed, if they can be repeated, if they are randomized so that each student's is different. A syllabus quiz encourages students to read the syllabus, and a lab-safety quiz reinforces safety concepts as well as encourages students to study their lab-safety materials more carefully.

- *Proctored exams*: Tell students how to find acceptable locations and individuals to administer a proctored exam and what kind of communication will be needed from or with individuals to qualify them to be proctors for examinations: "Unless you can come to campus on the prescribed exam date, you must arrange for an acceptable proctor to monitor your final exam. The proctor must be unrelated by family or friendship, certifiable as a responsible individual, agree to accept responsibility and comply with protocol directions, plus supervise your entire exam period. A librarian from your public or area high school library is a good choice. This person must call me from their work phone or e-mail me from their work e-mail address for verification and approval before proctoring instructions will be provided."

Net etiquette

This section should include a summary of the instructor's and the institution's rules and expectations regarding both online and offline interactions and the consequences for breach of these policies: "Any student who engages in inappropriate and disruptive communication may be dropped from the course, given a grade of F, and be ineligible for a tuition refund."

- Include rules about using proper professional English and punctuation, not text-message or twitter talk and not slang, abbreviations, or all upper- or lowercase letters.

- Instruct students to treat each other with respect and avoid communication that disrupts learning such as profanity, sexism, insults, threats, or harassing remarks.

- Include links to the student handbook, the institution's net etiquette policy, and netiquette websites such as www.albion.com/netiquette/

- State that the instructor reserves the right to delete messages which do not follow the guidelines.

Drop policy

Provide explicit details regarding your and institution's drop policy: "Students who fail to post to the discussion boards and/or submit assignments for two consecutive weeks will be dropped from the course." Reasons to drop a student might include inappropriate postings to the discussion boards or academic dishonesty.

Late policy and incompletes

Unless the course is fully self-paced, late policies should be structured to keep students on track and on time in completing assignments and the course. Once a student falls behind, it is very difficult to catch up. Few instructors, especially adjunct instructors, care to devote additional time to the work and documentation associated with allowing a student to finish an incomplete grade. Late and incomplete policies must be clearly specified. Most institutions' policies allow an Incomplete only for students who because of documented circumstances beyond their control are unable to complete their course work within the semester but have completed a majority (75–85%) of the course work and assignments with a C grade or better.

- Will assignments be accepted after their due date? If so, for how long and at what penalty?
- Will the instructor consider issuing a grade of Incomplete? If so, under what circumstances and for how long a period?

Plagiarism and academic dishonesty

Students should be sternly warned against cheating and risking their time and financial investment by engaging in plagiarism and academic dishonesty. (Chapter 6 discusses academic integrity in more detail.)

- Instructors need to clearly define these issues and provide details about the institution's policies and penalties for academic integrity infringements on all assignments, including lab reports.
- Because many students genuinely do not understand the fine line between referencing and plagiarizing information, they should be provided with examples and instructional websites to help them fully understand academic integrity issues.
- Students should also be advised that academic integrity and plagiarism software may be utilized to verify their work, including lab reports. This knowledge should motivate students to do original work and thus increase their level of learning.

Special accommodation and nondiscrimination

Include statements in compliance with institutional guidelines that reasonable accommodations can be made for students with physical and learning disabilities and that no student will be discriminated against on the basis of race, color, national or ethnic origin, religion, sex, or sexual orientation.

As in the first day of an on-campus lecture, the syllabus should also set a warm tone of welcome to help students feel comfortable in and excited about the class. It should also demonstrate the instructor's enthusiasm for science, stimulate the students' interest in the particular discipline, and make them proud of their decision to take the course (Frese, 2006).

INTERACTIVE PRESENTATIONS

To fully engage students in an online course, the materials should be as interactive as possible to address their different learning styles. Basically, three forms of interactions are possible in an online course: the students' interactions with the course content materials; the students' interactions with one another; and the students' interactions with the instructor. Other sections of this book address the latter two types of interactions. This section addresses the interactions of students with course content materials. These interactions represent a major challenge to instructors during the initial stages of moving their science courses online. This is when they must consider how to best present their course content in ways that will allow students with different learning styles to interact with and learn from the materials.

Interaction with the course material has to go beyond simply reading a textbook, writing a paper, and passing an exam. If a course provides nothing more than that, it is basically just an online correspondence course. Today's instructors have available a wide variety of user-friendly instructional tools to provide interactive elements to their online courses. Many of these technology tools are incorporated into existing LMS platforms and others are discussed in Chapter 3 of this book. Audio files, video clips, imbedded links, journal articles, simulations, and online tutorials that address the needs of auditory, visual, and kinesthetic learners are only a click and a download away.

Auditory learners tend to prefer chat rooms, video conference discussions, and broadcast case studies as learning tools. Podcasts, audio clips, and video clips with sound suit auditory learners. Supplement a lab science course's content with audiovideo clips and links to online lectures, such as the physics lectures by MIT professor Walter Lewin (http://web.mit.edu/physics/people/faculty/lewin_walter.html) appeal to auditory learners.

Visual learning content is easily added to online content. Lecture notes and PowerPoint slides should incorporate graphics, animated GIFs, Flash video, rollovers, and even simple simulations to captivate visual learners. However, to be effective, all these visual enhancements must relate to the course content and not simply be used to dress up the page.

Kinesthetic learners need to actively be involved with their course materials. Hands-on laboratory experiences can satisfy a lot of this need. Within the course materials, it is helpful to kinesthetic learners to literally move things around. Flash technology with drag-and-drop activities is effective in holding the attention of kinesthetic students.

Publishers for most textbooks adopted by online science instructors can provide an accompanying online course cartridge via a CD or a downloadable file containing a digital copy of the textbook plus course outlines, learning modules, study notes, problem sets, assessment instruments, and the like. These cartridges are normally uploaded into the LMS platform before the beginning of the term by an institution's IT personnel. If there is no IT department, the publisher will often help the instructor with installation to retain the adoption of their textbook.

Publishers' electronic course materials tend to be highly interactive. Adopting these materials is the fastest way to convert an online course into a dynamic interactive learning environment that is perfectly aligned with the textbook and various learning styles. These materials provide students with access to videos, online lectures, practice quizzes, and more. The only drawback is that these materials cannot be used without adopting the textbook. Depending upon the publisher and type of materials, the cost of such digital content may be included in the students' textbook price or assessed to the institution on a per-user basis.

Typically, the online course content is broken down into modules, and the related readings, course materials, discussion topics, assessments, and lab experiments are assigned one module at a time. The learning activities and materials for each learning module are often chunked, or broken down into shorter 10- to 15-minute subunits. These short sections allow students to break up their learning activities into blocks of time that better match their learning style and busy life.

There are numerous alternatives to traditional hard-copy textbooks for higher education. *Kindle* and emerging digital readers have further opened the door to online textbooks with interactive components. Video textbooks have been around for over a decade and are frequently used as primary or supplemental texts. The *Thinkwell* science series provides excellent interactive video lectures for all the science disciplines. Each series spans a full semester of traditional course topics and chunks the course materials into 10- to15-minute video segments. These digital video texts are great tools for both visual and auditory learners. Thinkwell previously provided these videos on DVDs but has recently moved their materials to servers that students can access to watch and study the materials online and also download PDF documents and video clips if they desire.

ONLINE DISCUSSION BOARDS

Online discussion boards help build a sense of community for an online course's students and enrich and expand their knowledge base, teamwork skills, and learning experiences. Discussion boards are invaluable tools that serve as social learning networks. They provide a forum where science students can meet, actively participate in the content of the course, and discuss related topics and their experimental results. Discussion boards help students keep up with the coursework and remind them to commence, complete, and submit their coursework on time. When science students encounter difficulties with course concepts, problems, or experiments, the discussion boards provide a place where they can go for help from both their peers and their professor. There, students find comfort and camaraderie with other students who share their challenges and with whom they can explore and share resources and findings.

The online community created through discussion boards encourages students to stay in class and to persevere when the going gets tough. It also stimulates and fosters healthy intellectual competition. Students race to contribute their thoughts, experiences, and research findings on their discussion boards. Their desire to be valuable, respected contributors to their course discussion boards motivates science students to exercise their best critical thinking skills. They strive to provide their peers and instructor with thoroughly considered, constructed, analyzed, and synthesized comments. Associate chemistry professor Venkat Chenobu (2007) of Jefferson Community College, part of the SUNY system, cites the quality of his online chemistry students' discussion board postings as evidence that they have a more profound and intimate experience of science than his F2F students. He states, "In the F2F situation, when a single answer is proposed for a question, that answer is usually embraced by the rest of the class and no more thinking occurs without intervention. In the online mode, everyone is thinking on their own."

It is recommended that science instructors establish at least three discussion boards:

- one for general course content and weekly discussion topics or questions
- one specifically dedicated to laboratory assignment discussions
- one to be used as a chat room for discussion of matters not related to the course

Normally, instructors track only participation in the general discussion board and use it for assessment purposes, but there is no reason the lab discussion board cannot also be tracked and graded.

General Course Discussion Board

The general course discussion board is the primary discussion board where course concepts and weekly discussion topics are explored and talked about. The instructor's requirements for the quantity and quality of students' discussion board participation should be explicitly defined along with the assessment criteria for participation and its impact on the final grade.

Most online science instructors define a posting as either a direct response to a discussion question or topic or a comment, question, or response related to another student's posting regarding that week's topic. Instructors usually require students to post at least one direct response to a weekly discussion topic and to comment on at least two postings submitted by different students. These postings are meant to expand the discussion beyond merely addressing the question or topic of the week. They should demonstrate genuine consideration of the topic, include elements of research, and stimulate further discussions. Students should be encouraged to read the science sections of major newspapers and to keep up with current science events related to the course discipline as this can provide great fodder for relevant and interesting discussions.

Typical online classes contain around 25 students, but such a large discussion group means students must read a lot of postings and can lose enthusiasm, focus, and interest. Similar to the contrast between conversations at large cocktail parties and small dinner gatherings, large group discussions tend toward the superficial and small groups tend toward intimate, relevant, and engaging discussions. For these reasons, it is frequently recommended online classes be divided into two or more groups for discussion board purposes.

The most common basis for this division is alphabetical, A though L in group 1 and M through Z in group 2, but this arbitrary assignment may create imbalances or disparities in the groups' dynamics. For this reason, some instructors wait until after the ice-breaking introductions to assign students to groups based on similar interests such as engineering and medical students or balancing the groups by ages, occupations, life experiences, and communication skills. Although changing group rosters later in the semester might be disruptive, instructors may want to consider this if there are underperforming teams.

Usually, students may, but are not required to, read the postings on the other groups' discussion board, but they may post responses and comments only in their own group's discussion board. If they read about something they want to discuss on the other board, they should post it on their own board to start a discussion there.

It is essential that an assessment rubric be posted so that students know exactly what is expected of their discussion board postings. The simple rubric described in Table 5.1 reflects common factors used to assess the quality of science discussion board postings. Typically, the instructor evaluates and assigns the points for discussion board postings, but some instructors allow students to evaluate one another's postings.

The first set of postings should be an icebreaker where the students introduce themselves to one another and to the instructor and then make comments and exchange information that will allow them to get to know one another better. Students should be encouraged to share their work and study schedules, which may facilitate online study groups. They should also be encouraged to exchange personal information and interests and tell why they are taking the specific science course, because this will help them identify others who share their interests. The personal information shared among students is also very valuable to science instructors, because it gives them a basis for developing examples and explanations that will be specifically relevant and meaningful to the students.

The general discussion board is also the gathering point for general exchanges about course content. This is where students can post their general questions, brilliant thoughts, or substantial scientific findings discovered during their research. Instructors should feel free to also contribute to the discussion board, respond to students' comments, offer links to interesting articles, and provide study tips and guidelines when appropriate. However, instructors should avoid the urge to jump in and promptly respond to students' questions as soon as they are posted. Wait a few

Table 5.1.
Rubric for Assessment of Required
Weekly Postings to Discussion Boards

Unsatisfactory: 0 points	Needs Work: 6 points	Satisfactory: 8 points	Very Good: 10 points
Fewer than three postings	Three or more simple postings	Three or more thoughtful postings	Three or more thoughtful and substantive postings
	Postings are too brief or of poor quality.	Postings have at least three sentences expressing valid points.	Postings have three or more sentences creatively expressing valid, well-argued points supported by evidence.
	(a) Postings are *not* very thoughtful or substantive or fail to address related topic *or* (b) Postings fail to respond to two fellow students, or responses are simplistic and lack adequate thought and details.	(a) Postings thoughtfully, substantively, and fully address related topic *or* (b) Postings adequately respond to two fellow students with responses that reflect thoughtful consideration and adequate details.	(a) Postings also reference outside resource or relevant, real-world examples or applications. *or* (b) Posting in response to classmate clearly states position in relation to classmate's comments.

hours. In all likelihood other students will quickly offer their thoughts and assistance on the matter, will probably do just as good if not a better job than the instructor, and will have a richer learning experience from having solved the problem among themselves. However, an instructor should not hesitate to jump in if the students are going down a wrong path and need a bit of guidance to get back on track.

The majority of postings to the general course discussion board will be about the week's discussion question or topic. To avoid late postings that allow no time for comments or rebuttals, students should be instructed to post their initial responses to the science question or topic of the week no later than midweek. This leaves the balance of the week and adequate time for responses and lively subsequent discussions to take place.

What types of questions make good discussion board topics? Science certainly presents numerous challenging and interesting topics for discussion, but selecting and framing questions that excite students' interest and stimulate great online discussion is not always easy. It is important that discussion questions are relevant to the students as well as to the course content and that they elicit the higher-level thinking skills of Bloom's taxonomy.

A question that can be answered with a simple yes or no should never be asked. Nor should students be asked only if they agree or disagree with a statement. It is much better to ask about the intent of a statement and the students' point of view regarding its validity.

One possibility for the general discussion board is to start with an outrageous statement or a provocative claim such as "Global warming must be a myth because we continue to have major snow storms in Colorado." Today's tabloid and television media are replete with pseudoscience articles and programming such as *Ghost Stories* by Fox Cable TV and *Ghost Lab* as well as other paranormal programming by the Discovery Channel. Even major national networks often feature sensationalist stories about Big Foot, UFOs, haunted houses, and the Loch Ness Monster as though they were based upon scientific fact. It is fun to occasionally post discussion questions about the pseudoscience on television and in the tabloids and to ask students if the science behind the claims is reasonable and to explain why or why not.

A similar line of questions can be asked about movies that contain science components which are wrong or misleading such as Indiana Jones blithely handling a sculptured head supposedly made of solid gold when such an object in reality would be too heavy to easily lift. Students don't usually question inconsistencies or impossibilities they see in films until they are pointed out, but then they begin to think more critically about things they see. Lively and enlightening discussions often ensue as students begin to recall movie scenes and discuss which scientific laws were broken or what facts were ignored in them.

Starting a general discussion board with a Fermi question and encouraging students to construct their own Fermi questions is a good way to set the stage for science learning and build critical thinking skills. Of course, this type of question does not expect an exact answer; rather it is designed to expose the problem-solver's thinking processes. Here's sample wording for a typical Fermi question posed in physics:

> Famous physicist and Nobel Price winner Enrico Fermi said good scientists should be able to answer any problem posed to them. They may not necessarily produce the correct answer, but they should develop an algorithm that allows an order-of-magnitude estimate to be obtained based on things they either know or that can be reliably estimated. Our discussion topic for Chapter 1 is based on a question Fermi often asked on undergraduate physics exams: "How many piano tuners are there in Chicago at any given time?" To make it relevant to the majority of you who live in Colorado, let's rephrase the question. "How many piano tuners are there in Denver at any given time?"

Another approach that students enjoy is to use homework problems as a basis for discussion. Here each student is assigned different homework problems for which they must post the full details of their step-by-step approach and rationale in arriving at a solution. Then they must respond to three other students' postings; responses may involve a different approach or a potential correction. Students enjoy this process because they are not required to solve all assigned problems. However, they must invest substantial energy in composing their solution for posting and then closely review the posted solutions of other students, so they are still exposed to all homework problems and usually have a more meaningful learning experience.

Although net etiquette should be covered thoroughly in the course syllabus, the instructor should reiterate basic guidelines for civil discourse when making initial discussion board assignments. Students should be reminded that they do not always have to agree with each other—after all, disagreements often provide food for thought—but they do always have to treat one another with respect. If a student posts anything inappropriate on a discussion board, the instructor should privately point out to the student exactly what was improper about the posting and request the student to post a retraction or apology if appropriate. Although students are rarely too verbose in their discussion board postings, to avoid this problem instructors may wish to place a 500-word or other limit on the length of each post.

At the end of a discussion period, science instructors should formally bring the discussion to a close before moving on to the next question or topic. The main points made and solutions covered during each discussion period should be summarized for reinforcement. Instructors often assign this task to students on a rotating basis.

Lab Discussion Board

Questions about lab experiments can easily get lost and be overlooked in the numerous postings to a general course discussion board. Students working on their laboratory experiments at home certainly don't want their questions overlooked or to wait days for a response. A specific lab discussion board is where they can post all questions, responses, and comments regarding their lab work and experimental findings.

Most lab discussion board postings relate to uncertainties regarding experimental procedures and results. Instructors should restrain themselves from responding too quickly. Procedural questions are usually best left to other science students for response because those students may having similar experiences and problems and can relate to one another's questions and issues. Further, students like to be helpful. It makes them feel good and cements group relationships, and providing information to others reinforces that information for oneself. Here's an illustrative example of two physics students' interaction on a lab discussion board:

> *Student #1:* I'm having trouble determining how to set up the circuit with the ammeter for Parts 2 and 3. A detailed example on how to include the ammeter in the circuit would be helpful. For instance, Procedure D in Part 2 says to measure current through each resistor at each of the marked points. Great. I see where they want it measured, but I'm lost as to how the cables and leads are organized. Any advice?
>
> *Student #2:* Go back to the Intro to Electrical Circuits lab. It covers this and has pictures. The ammeter has to be part of the circuit. You must connect an alligator wire to the battery terminal and connect one lead of the ammeter to the other end of the alligator wire. Then you attach another wire to the second lead of the ammeter and connect it to the resistor, etc. If that doesn't help I'll try to take a photo for you.
>
> *Student #1:* Thanks, I forgot about those photos in the manual. Now I see my mistake.

Chat Discussion Board

Establishing a chat discussion board provides an area where students can go to talk about topics of personal interest that are not related to the course. It serves the same purpose as a student lounge on campus and is a place where online students can simply hang out if they wish. Again, net etiquette should be reinforced, but this can be done with an informal initial reminder to keep the conversations "clean and civil." Instructors may wish to periodically review the postings to chat discussion boards, but they should avoid posting any comments of their own unless absolutely necessary, because this area should be a personal and safe zone for the students.

Promoting Academic Integrity in Online Science Courses

A 1998 survey from *Who's Who Among American High School Students* reported that of 3,123 students, 80% of them "admitted to cheating on an exam." This represented a 10-point increase since the question was first asked 15 years earlier (Bushweller, 1999). In addition, 50% of the students who admitted cheating "did not believe cheating was necessarily wrong," and 95% of those who had cheated said they have never been caught (Kleiner & Lord, 1999).

According to the Center for Academic Integrity at Duke University, 75% of all college students "confess to cheating at least once" (Kleiner & Lord, 1999). This finding confirms earlier studies by Baird and by Stern and Havlicek, who reported that 70% to 85% of American college students "engaged in some form of cheating" (as cited in Lupton, Chapman, & Weiss, 2000).

These studies imply that that almost every student cheats, and the inference is that they cheat all the time and in all their classes. Although it is not surprising that most students have cheated at some time in their lives, confessing to a single incident of cheating at some time in the past does not mean that a student was or is a continuous, serial cheater in every course he or she takes. Together, we have taught almost half a century on campus and online, and we do not believe that the brazen dishonesty implied by the reported statistics are inherently true nor that wide-scale cheating is as rampant as implied.

Because students were cheating in classrooms under the watchful eyes of instructors long before online instruction came of age, the increased suspicions of academic dishonesty among unsupervised online students is not surprising. To examine the cheating issue and gauge the extent of academic integrity among his variously situated chemistry students, Dr. Peter Jeschofnig conducted several studies between 2002 and 2006. These studies encompassed his on-campus, video-conferencing, and online chemistry courses at Colorado Mountain College. Each class was given two strictly proctored exams toward the beginning of the semester. Throughout the semester, chemistry students from all groups were given unsupervised take-home exams and quizzes. At the end of the semester another strictly proctored exam was given to all students (Jeschofnig, 2006).

Interestingly, there was no material change in grade distribution among the different types of classes. Each class's students made the same level of grades on their take-home exams that they made on their strictly proctored exams. Students who did poorly, barely passed, or failed the proctored exams consistently achieved similarly poor results on their take-home exams regardless of how their courses were taught. If extensive cheating had been taking place in any of these classes, the students who had made very poor grades on their proctored exams should have shown marked improvement in the grades for their unsupervised take-home exams. The fact that there was no improvement in grades when there was the opportunity for cheating implies that no serious cheating had taken place in any of the three types of courses.

Theoretically, the potential for cheating is substantially greater for unsupervised students taking an online course than for students taking courses in supposedly supervised campus settings. Yet, just because it is easier to cheat in an online course, does that mean online students are more likely to cheat? Several recent studies unequivocally refute that assumption and, conversely, show that cheating is actually less prevalent among online students (Wherry and Lundberg, 2009; Stuber-McEwen, Wiselye, & Hoggartt, 2009). It is interesting to speculate upon the cause for higher academic integrity in online classes and whether it is related to the demographics of online students, who appear to be more mature individuals with focused career goals.

Many science instructors continue to believe online cheating is a major problem because among the initial questions they usually ask when moving courses online is how to prevent cheating. Regardless of whether or not there is more academic dishonesty in online courses, the fact is that this perception is plausible and pervasive. This makes it incumbent on online educators to protect the integrity of their courses by using every means possible to discourage and detect academic dishonest. Fortunately, there are several excellent ways to do this.

SET THE STAGE FOR ACADEMIC INTEGRITY

An instructor should set the stage for academic integrity by directly addressing the issues of cheating and plagiarism in the course syllabus. It should inform students of expected academic standards for scholarship and conduct, clearly explain what constitutes cheating and plagiarism, and provide references and links to sites that elaborate on this topic. Science instructors should also appeal to students' better side by moralizing a bit about how cheating harms society as well as the students and how high moral standards benefit everyone and make the world a better place. They should specifically discuss the vital importance of integrity to scientific work and research and the consequences to society if scientists do not honestly and ethically pursue their research and report their scientific findings.

Students should be made aware that their work is subject to examination by anti-plagiarism software and internal comparisons, and they should be told about the sanctions and punishments that will be enforced against those who succumb to dishonesty. Because collaboration is encouraged or allowed on many assignments, each assignment should clearly be labeled whether it is to be performed independently and represent only the student's work or whether it may be performed in collaboration with others.

The direct discussions science instructors have with individual students via e-mails and discussion board postings can also promote academic integrity, as well as detect problems. Instructors can build bonds of trust with students by respectfully listening to them and personally responding to their comments and concerns. Human nature is such that having a trusting relationship with a respected and respectful individual tends to make one want to merit that person's respect and trust. Also, these exchanges familiarize science instructors with each student's capabilities and better enable the instructors to recognize when students' assessed work exceeds those levels and may not be their own. For example, a red flag would arise if a perfectly worded and grammatically correct research paper was submitted by a student whose interactions with the instructor had reflected less than perfect written language abilities.

Instructors should also have students submit clear scanned copies of their photo ID along with a picture of themselves holding the photo ID. This helps to confirm the student taking the course is actually the student enrolled, and there's also a psychological propensity toward being honest with people who have seen one's face. The photo ID may also serve as a useful reference later in the semester, especially if the instructor utilizes proctored exams or requires students to submit photos of themselves performing their lab work, a recommended practice.

It is extremely important that science instructors noticeably and transparently set and monitor an expectation for high standards of academic integrity in their courses. They must take visible actions to deter and detect dishonesty and make certain their students are aware that cheating will not be tolerated. If cheating is suspected but cannot be fully proved, the instructor should directly inform the student of the reasons why his or her work is suspect and that his or her work will be examined even more closely in the future. This may deter a student with a propensity to cheat. If a science instructor believes beyond a reasonable doubt that cheating has occurred, the instructor must act immediately to enforce the disciplinary actions described in the course syllabus.

The following sections provide information and tips on preventing and detecting academic dishonesty. Another, albeit old-fashioned, way of ensuring a student has not been cheating and really knows the course material is by means of an oral exam. Other than in graduate school, oral exams are seldom used for assessment of learning today, but they provide the online science instructor with firsthand knowledge about a student's understanding of course concepts and are thus an excellent way to determine if a student has been cheating. Schedule a telephone conference with the suspected student for a sufficient length of time and compile specific questions to ask that are directly related to information the student should know if he or she performed the course work. The result of an oral exam can move an instructor from suspicion to certainty regarding a student's guilt or innocence.

TOOLS TO PREVENT OR REDUCE CHEATING

There are numerous approaches a science instructor can use that will help to prevent or at least reduce cheating in online classes. It is best to have all assignments submitted by students processed through the course's LMS platform. Students have unique LMS login passwords, so there is at least assurance that the materials are coming through the student's portal. Additionally, this immediately alerts the instructor of missing submittals at their cutoff date, and it facilitates grading of assignments and assessments as well as posting of grades and computing grade averages in the grade book.

A variety of exam types are available from an LMS. Assessments can be created in the form of essays, numeric problems, and short written responses, which the instructor can evaluate personally or have the system automatically grade according to "key word" markers. Assessments can also take the form of traditional multiple-choice, true/false, ordering, or other objective types of questions. Such objective assessments are automatically graded by the system upon their completion, and the results are immediately entered in the grade book and displayed for students' review; this allows the students to see their grade as well as review where they made mistakes.

Objective assessment questions can be created and uploaded into the LMS by the instructor; however, this can be a fairly time-consuming chore. Many instructors prefer to use the extensive objective test banks provided by textbook publishers in their course cartridges. These test questions are organized and identified by chapter, module, or learning objective and can be selected and combined in a variety of different assessments. Some best practices for using test banks to prevent or minimize cheating include the following.

Timed and Randomly Generated Exams

LMS platforms provide science instructors with a plethora of options for the organization and presentation of exams and quizzes. Randomized exams can take two forms. A fixed number of random questions by learning objective can be generated from the test bank, or all students can be given the exact same questions, but the LMS is directed to deliver them in different randomized order to each student; thus no two students should receive an exam that is exactly the same in all respects. Randomizing the questions prevents students from getting a valid answer if they call a friend asking "What did you get for number 8?" because number 8 will be different for each of them. Yet if all students receive the same questions, just in randomized order, this allows for genuine evaluation and comparison of the exam and student scores and identification of problem areas.

For problem-solving questions, some LMS assessment software is now able to ask identical questions to all students but to generate a different data set for each student's problems. Thus, all students are tested on the same concepts, and blatant cheating will be conspicuously exposed.

An instructor can also instruct the LMS to set the amount of time allowed for each exam as well as set parameters such as these: if the exam can be interrupted and returned to at a later time; if it can be taken multiple times; and if it can be copied or printed. Reasonable but tightly controlled timing for exams prevents students from being able to look up answers in the text or call a friend for a lifeline. Students should not be able to copy, print, or interrupt their taking of important exams because this opens the door for suspicion of dishonesty. Students should be clearly advised in advance about the time limits for each exam along with all other restrictions so that they can schedule an uninterrupted period that will allow them to complete all questions in one sitting.

Instructors can also create exams with questions that require substantial critical thought and research to complete. The deadline for submittal of these exams should give students adequate time to perform the work, but not enough time for them to farm out the task to someone else—24 hours is normally adequate. Taking this type of exam also serves as a learning and knowledge-reinforcing tool.

It is also possible for science instructors to use the LMS's course-tracking data to perform their own integrity analysis by running a correlation between individual students' exam grades and the amounts of time spent on an exam versus the class averages. Although an abnormal correlation would not be proof of cheating, if, for example, a student made an A on a science exam expected to take at least an hour to complete but spent only 15 minutes taking the exam, then cheating should certainly be suspected and other course components should be investigated to verify suspicions.

Proctored Exams

Proctored exams may be a bit more difficult to implement for online courses, but they are not impossible. Online students unable to take proctored exams on campus should be required to secure proctors who are willing and able to administer the exam and are acceptable to the instructor. Librarians are usually reliable individuals willing to assume this responsibility. In the unlikely event that no librarians are available to handle this task, another respected authority figure in the community can be used, provided that he or she is not related to the student by family or friendship. Students in the military should be able to find a commanding officer to accept this duty.

The instructor should verify all proctors' credentials and provide them with detailed instructions regarding their responsibilities in supervising and administering the exam. These responsibilities must include obtaining and verifying a photo ID of the student taking the exam and submitting a copy of the verified ID to the instructor with the exam documents. The instructor must also arrange to securely transmit the exam to the proctor and to have its results securely transmitted back. The easiest way to do this is to have the students take the proctored exam online via the course's LMS platform. The instructor then only needs to send a password to the proctor, who will use it to open the password-protected exam when the student and proctor are ready to commence. Because the completed exam will be stored in the LMS, no additional paperwork other than the copy of the student's ID needs to be exchanged between the instructor and proctor.

Research Papers

When a science research paper is required, online instructors have to deal with the same honesty issues as campus instructors. They may wonder if plagiarism was involved or if the paper was perhaps purchased from one of many Internet services. Fortunately, a lot of good software is available for checking papers for plagiarism. Many upgraded LMS platforms now have plagiarism checks such as Turn It In built into their system, and these can be used to evaluate all types of student submittals. Because "passed-on" papers tend to come from within institutions, it is a good idea for instructors to create their own database of papers for evaluating future papers for plagiarism via software such as Viper. Instructors should save and pool their students' formal papers with those of other instructors offering the same courses to create an institution-wide database.

For the ultimate in assurance of academic integrity, instructors can employ some of today's super-sleuthing security technology. Some use dedicated browsers that are locked into the exam system so that students cannot perform online searches while taking an exam. Also available are affordable fish-eye-view cameras with fingerprint scan and verification technology. *Securexam*'s Remote Proctor is an example of this kind of hardware. It is installed on the student's computer and then interfaced into an online monitoring system that monitors and records all movements in the entire at-home exam room. Proposed federal mandates to prevent cheating in online courses will no doubt increase the availability and decrease the cost of such technologies in the future.

ELIMINATE THE NECESSITY FOR DISHONESTY

A good way to eliminate dishonesty in lab science courses is to simply take away the incentive to cheat and at the same time utilize assessments as teaching and reinforcement tools—especially objective quizzes and interim exams. These types of exams can be organized to not display the same questions on each attempt at the assessment, but rather to display different questions related to the same learning objectives for each attempt. The instructor places no time restrictions on such exams and allows students to retake them as often as desired. Students are encouraged to research questions that they missed or are uncertain about before reattempting the exam. However, students should know that only the grade for their last attempt at the exam will be entered into the grade book.

When science students review their graded exams, they will be able to see where they made mistakes. Then it is expected that they will perform research to understand their mistakes and to correct their misunderstandings. Thus, their next attempt at the assessment should reflect improved knowledge of the subject matter. These are the assumptions behind utilizing multiple and open assessments as teaching tools:

- Students will feel no need to cheat because they have ample opportunity to research and discover the correct answers themselves and can then eliminate similar mistakes on a subsequent attempt at the assessment.

- As a result of their own corrective processes, science students should genuinely learn the course materials.

MINIMIZE AND DETECT CHEATING ON LAB WORK AND LAB REPORTS

It is assumed that science instructors will require their students to compile and submit formal written lab reports for at least 50% of their lab assignment. Lab reports can contain several clues that might generate suspicion that a student has "borrowed" from another's lab report. A student's writing style on discussion boards should be similar to that in his or her written lab reports. For example, if a nonnative-English-speaking student is suddenly writing lab reports in perfect English prose, that is cause for suspicion and further investigation.

Another source of clues is a comparison of the results recorded in students' data tables. Traditional experimental procedures require observing, quantifying, recording, and manipulating measurement data to at least two decimal places. Given the nature of experimentation and science measurements, it is fairly unlikely that two students' data will reflect exactly the same quantities. Two students reporting the exact quantitative data in their lab reports is not prima facie evidence of cheating, but it does indicate that further investigation may be needed.

Here are additional suggestions to prevent and detect cheating/plagiarism on lab reports:

• Require students to submit photos of themselves with their lab setups as part of each lab report. All students have digital cameras if not cell phones containing digital cameras, so this should not be an inconvenient burden. Assuming photo IDs were requested at the beginning of the semester, these lab photos can be compared to those IDs to ascertain that the registered student is the same student in the lab photo. Granted, a student can be pictured with an experimental procedure and still not have performed the lab work, but if students go to that much trouble, there is a high probability that they will also engage in some of the experimentation activities.

• Penny Perkins of California State University, San Marcos has taken a giant leap forward with photography in her online anatomy and physiology classes. She has each student compile a short video lab report at the conclusion of performing each experiment. The student is instructed to play the role of teacher and visually depict as well as verbally report the actions they took, the results they achieved, and the conclusions they made. Students enjoy having the creative opportunity to produce, direct, and star in their own films. The performance of experimental activities has more relevance to students because they know they must perform them well in order to teach them to their instructor.

Perkins believes her online students' understanding of their course materials is higher than for any other kinds of classes she has taught. She attributes the requirement to create instructional lab videos with solidifying the knowledge students gain through their experimentation activities. Further, because a picture is worth a thousand words, Perkins (2010) is reasonably confident that students who submit video lab reports in which they are depicted have actually done their own work.

Most lab science manuals include questions that students should address within their lab reports. Because lab manuals are often used for several successive years, the answers to these questions may be passed on by prior students. To get around this potential problem, add new lab question sets each semester or use different data sets for the questions asked.

• It is also useful to have lab quizzes following each experiment and a final lab exam. The questions should be difficult or impossible to answer by anyone who has not actually performed the lab experiments.

• If the course requires the student to purchase a lab kit to complete the laboratory component of the course, it is important to ascertain that each student has actually obtained his or her science lab kit. Obviously, it is not possible for students to complete their lab exercises without the assigned lab kit. Thus it is a best practice for kit-adopting science instructors to have their students submit a copy of their kit purchase receipt. Alternatively, after the course census date, it is possible to request and match the class rosters against the lab kit vendor's list of purchasers. Upon request, for example, Hands-On Labs will provide science instructors with a list of students who have purchased LabPaqs for their courses. Possession of a lab kit does not guarantee that students will actually perform their lab work, but because lab kits are not cheap, it is likely that students who purchase them will actually perform their own lab work and not waste such an expensive investment.

• The same kind of anti-plagiarism software and LMS checks used for formal papers can be used for lab reports. Again, creating an internal data bank of department- or institution-wide lab submittals is very helpful.

STUDENT TRACKING DATA

One of the most useful features of an LMS platform is its student tracking feature. This feature follows and records students' course participation in several ways and provides reports requested by the science instructor. Depending on the LMS used, the following tracking and reporting features may be available.

First and Last Access Dates

This reveals a student's initial and most recent access dates to the online course materials. At the beginning of the semester, it lets the science instructor know whether a student has started the course. Later in the semester, it informs the instructor whether the student is continuing to access the course materials.

Access dates are very useful information, especially during the first few weeks of the course. It allows instructors to identify students who have not yet started the course or frequently accessed the materials. They should contact AWOL students to make certain they have the required course materials, information, and passwords and know how to access and navigate the course content. Instructors should determine if the students genuinely understand what is expected of them or if they have any technical problems. They should remind these students of the danger of falling behind, and in general let them know that there is a concerned educator who cares about their learning success and is available to help them.

The last access date lets the instructor know if a student has stopped submitting assignments but has not formally withdrawn from the class or advised the instructor of his or her intentions. Typically, this type of withdrawal will result in a grade of F. Usually, when submitting a grade of F, the instructor is asked to provide a last participation date. Because there is no weekly class roll, the LMS's last access date can serve that purpose. Occasionally, a student is enrolled in a class through an administrative mistake. Having information that confirms the course was never accessed will bolster such a claim.

Total Number of Visits

This data is more an indicator of a student's study habits and may not actually be of great significance or have any implications regarding cheating. One student may log on into the LMS only once or twice a week to download and upload pertinent course materials, whereas another student may prefer to log in daily or even multiple times a day. The quality of science students' work depends more on total time and effort expended on studying than on how often they log into the course.

Average Time per Visit

The average time science students spend per visit has a bit more relevance but only when considered along with personal knowledge of an individual student and his or her computer habits. Students whose first language is not English may spend considerably more time online than native English speakers because they read and comprehend English text more slowly. Some students may log into the course only long enough to download all pertinent material into their own computer and then read and study those materials and do all their online research outside of the LMS. Conversely, other students may read all of the course content directly online and perform all their Internet research from inside the LMS.

Where this feature's data may be extremely useful is in reviewing online quiz and exam results. Did someone who failed an exam spend 15 minutes or two hours with the exam? Students who spend only 15 minutes on a two-hour exam obviously did not make an effort, and any complaints about their grade will carry little weight. However, if a failing student struggled to complete the exam, his or her perseverance indicates a desire to succeed that might be facilitated with direct intervention or tutoring by the science instructor. As noted earlier, the time spent taking an exam can also be an indication of cheating. If a science student whose discussion board comments are less than stellar surprisingly completes a very difficult exam in record time and makes an A on it, an instructor would have a solid basis for suspecting the student of dishonesty.

Total Time

The total amount of time each student has spent in online sessions may not have a lot of relevance, but it is useful to compare these numbers for several students to see if there is any correlation to performance.

Pages Visited

This feature helps identify which online LMS tools and pages students are using and not using. If a student is doing poorly in the course, the instructor can see if the student is not accessing lecture notes, PowerPoints, or other pages containing important references and beneficial information. This observation can then be brought to the student's attention along with directions to those specific resources that will help the student with his or her science studies. This type of intervention shows students that their instructor is paying attention to them and cares about their performance. When employed early in the semester, it can help get wayward science students on the right track and motivate them to put more effort into learning the course materials.

When looking at student tracking data, it is important for science instructors to not jump to conclusions. For example, a short login time is not necessarily explained by lack of engagement. This may simply mean that the student is printing, downloading, or saving the materials to read offline. A long session time does not necessarily mean that a student spent the entire time engaging with the resource. They could be using a very old computer or a slow modem or have a slow Internet connection; they may not be native English speakers and need more time to make sense of the course material; or they may have interrupted their work to do something else and simply did not log out of the LMS.

Typical LMS Tracking Data

First and last access dates	Number of assessments completed
How many logins	Total time spent on online assessments
Total time logged in	Number of assignments read
Number of e-mail messages read	Number of assignments submitted
Number of e-mail messages sent	Number of content pages viewed
Number of discussion messages read	
Number of discussion messages posted	Number of web links used
Number of times calendar was accessed	Number of files viewed

Tracking the quantity of time spent within an LMS and the patterns of science students' usage of their resource materials is helpful in identifying when an intervention may be needed and in evaluating a suspicion of cheating. This tracking data should be used to identify students at risk of falling behind, dropping out, or failing the course and to quickly offer assistance and encouragement when needed. Science instructors should run herd on their students by encouraging them to complete their studies and submit their assignments on time. Tracking students' frequency of access and length of time spent with specific LMS pages does not indicate the quality of the student's engagement with it. With the possible exception of discussion board activity, LMS tracking data should not be used to assess students' performance or to modify their grades.

The Art of Incorporating Online Lab Assignments

Just as online courses are dramatically changing educational delivery, they are also dramatically changing academic calendars. Students are no longer confined to taking courses only during the three conventional semesters conducted in spring, summer, and fall. Most colleges now offer online courses over multiple semesters spanning 15, 12, 10, or 8 weeks and even intensive 4-week semesters. Some colleges, such as Western Governor's University, allow students to begin a course of study on the first day of any month of the year. It and numerous other emerging online colleges allow students to work at their own pace, so there is no specific time frame allocated to their course.

HOW MANY EXPERIMENTS TO PERFORM

Conscientious lab science instructors fear overburdening their online students and wonder if they should offer fewer labs in online courses where students do not have direct instructional supervision or in courses conducted over a shortened semester. Because the purpose of science laboratory experimentation is to illustrate, clarify, and reinforce major course concepts, the location or duration of a lab science course should not determine the quantity or the type of lab work assigned. Only the course content should do that. Students who choose to take a lab science course online or within a condensed or expanded time frame should still be required to do the same quantity and quality of lab work as those who take a traditional F2F course on campus over a typical semester. Students should be advised of the approximate time they will need to devote to lab work, but how they choose to schedule this work is their concern, not that of their instructor's.

Instead of assigning science lab work by setting arbitrary time periods, as much as possible lab work timing should be guided by the need to correspond lab work with coverage of course learning objectives. The delivery mode of instruction or the length of the course should not dictate lab timing criteria; rather, the focus should be on the number of credit hours assigned to the course's lab component and the approximate amount of time normally required to complete the experiments associated with learning the course's concepts.

Online lab science instructors should consider the time they expect students to devote to traditional F2F lab sessions over the typical 15-week academic term as a lab assignment guide for online courses. Depending upon the course discipline and the type of experiments performed, this normally spans 12 weeks of lab sessions at two to eight hours per week. Instructors can use this total time as a gauge for assigning equivalent lab work in online lab science courses, but they must remember to adjust for experiment assignments that require considerably longer or shorter times than average.

It's also possible to link the quantity of lab work assigned to the course's allocated science lab credits as well as the normal time associated with earning those credits. At the undergraduate level and depending upon the science discipline and its program level, students may engage in two, four, or eight hours of science lab work for each hour of academic credit earned. On average, a one-credit science lab course incorporates 24 to 72 total lab work hours over the online term, and a two-credit lab course incorporates 48 to 96 total lab work hours. Science instructors should select the appropriate type and number of experiments that can be completed within these average time frames regardless of the mode or length of the course.

USING COMPUTER SIMULATIONS WITH ONLINE SCIENCE COURSES

In the early days of online science teaching, the lab component was often based entirely on computer simulations, which were then thought to be the panacea of the online lab predicament. However, it did not take long before professional organizations including the American Chemical Society and the National Science Teachers Association as well as many colleges, universities, and employers began to evaluate and question the learning effectiveness of virtual labs as acceptable replacements for 100% of traditional hands-on laboratory experiences (ACS, 2009).

Some proponents of lab simulations have insisted that simulations are in fact a valid substitute for wet labs because "a significant fraction of students go through wet laboratories with little thought about what they should learn, but narrowly follow the written directions for and experiment to get the expected results (affectionately called 'cookbooking')" (Woodfield et al., 2004). Woodfield and his colleagues further suggest that "a prime factor behind this tendency to cookbook is the rigidity imposed upon instructional laboratories by severe time constraints, large numbers of students, costs, environmental considerations, and safety considerations."

One of the most serious shortcomings of computer laboratory simulations is that they cannot effectively teach laboratory techniques and lab safety. Clicking a computer mouse to instantaneously dispense exactly 25 ml of a chemical into a graphic beaker is not the same as carefully measuring out the same 25 ml with a graduated cylinder or a pipette. Such simulated experiences do not allow students to make valuable learning errors or require them to add or remove a few drops of chemical and genuinely understand the importance of exact measurements as they verify the meniscus is properly considered. Similarly, a virtual dissection with perfect incisions and vividly illustrated organs does not present biology students with the ambiguities they must learn to overcome in observing actual tissue. With simulations, students cannot personally experience the odor, color, viscosity, and other properties of the science materials they must handle. Fear that lab simulations cannot replicate genuine science learning and teach safe lab techniques is among the primary reasons many colleges will no longer accept 100% simulation-based lab science course credits. However, creative instructors aware of simulation's shortcomings may be able to devise exercises to help mitigate these.

These drawbacks do not mean that computer lab simulations have no place in distance science learning. Simulations can be useful as a pre-lab to hands-on wet labs and to help prepare students to perform actual tactile experiments. As post-labs, they can reinforce and clarify the concepts learned in tactile labs. Simulations are also valid substitutes for experiments that are too expensive or too dangerous to be performed hands-on. Further, virtual labs may be the only option available to some online instructors, and a simulated laboratory experience is certainly better for online science students than no laboratory experiences at all.

When used as a pre-lab, simulations can partially replace pre-lab briefings. They introduce science students to the way tactile experiments are performed, allow students to try a larger number of virtual combinations, encourage students' participation in the design of experiments, and build confidence in their ability to perform the actual experiment. Performing virtual laboratory simulations can give science students sufficient procedural understanding and confidence to correctly perform future wet-lab experiments on their first try and eliminate the need to repeat the experiments because of procedural errors. Thus, using simulations as pre-lab experiences can save materials, eliminate waste, and minimize errors when the experiment is actually performed.

There are many examples where virtual simulations have been successfully used as a supplement to hands-on labs. Several years ago Dr. Peter Jeschofnig taught a hybrid online organic chemistry class at Colorado Mountain College. The lecture portion of the class was delivered 100% online and the hands-on lab component was delivered via bimonthly, all-day Saturday laboratory sessions. Students often drove over a hundred miles to attend the lab sessions, but severe weather across high mountain passes occasionally made traveling impossible. Students forced to miss a lab sessions were allowed to complete the missed lab assignments through Woodfield's Organic Virtual ChemLabs software, which will be discussed shortly (with sample screens shown in Figure 7.1). This combination of hands-on labs interspersed with a few simulations worked very well, and on an anecdotal basis, it appeared to genuinely boost students understanding of organic chemistry concepts.

Dr. Paul Vorndam, the science chair for CCCOnline, previously used virtual simulations with his online introductory chemistry courses. He had satisfactory experiences with both Model Science Software, which is delivered via a purchased software download, and with Late Nite Labs, which is now delivered solely online via purchased access codes. Each provides a menu of experiment titles from which he selected and assigned experiments to match his course objectives just as he identifies and selects hands-on experiments for his campus-based tactile lab sessions. Although today he employs commercially

Figure 7.1.
Examples from Woodfield's Virtual ChemLabs

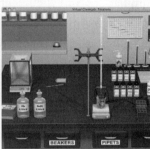

assembled lab kits because he believes hands-on labs provide a better learning experience, he still occasionally uses laboratory simulations as pre- and post-lab aids. His ideal lab learning experience for students would consist of a pre-lab simulation, followed by a video demonstration of each experiment's set-up and procedures, and culminated by hands-on manipulation and observations of related science materials (L. Jeschofnig, personal communication, August 29, 2009).

Numerous commercial simulations for purchase as well as free simulations are available for most science disciplines. Public institutions and dedicated professors readily share their simulations via free downloads from their websites, but these are not usually of the best quality. A Google search for discipline-specific science lab simulations will produce a large number of hits. Experienced lab science educators will have no problem testing and evaluating the appropriateness of the various simulation offerings for their disciplines.

Among the better simulations in chemistry are Woodfield's *Virtual ChemLab* projects. They are available on CD for general chemistry and organic chemistry courses, are sold through several publishers, and can also be purchased from online sites.

A good source of quality lab simulations for both chemistry and biology is *Late Nite Labs* (LNL; http://www.latenitelabs.com). These are today delivered only online via both institutional subscriptions and direct student purchases. Links for institutions, instructors and students are managed by LNL.

Model Science Software (http://www.modelscience.com) produces chemistry simulations and is currently developing virtual labs for biology and physics. Downloads for these fairly simplistic but easy-to-use lab simulations are purchased online by students. Figure 7.2 shows a sample screen.

Depicted in Figures 7.3 and 7.4 are a couple of free, downloadable chemistry simulations. Obviously, their graphics are not as sophisticated as the commercial simulations. However, they still allow students to see the what, when, and why of the experiment.

The *Howard Hughes Medical Institute* (www.hhmi.org/biointeractive/vlabs/index.html) has developed several free and very useful virtual labs in biology, which include *The Bacterial Identification Lab* and *The Neurophysiology Lab.*

Biology Labs On-line (http://www.biologylab.awlonline.com) is a commercial website created via collaboration between the California State University system and Benjamin Cummings, an imprint of Pearson Education, Inc. It offers a series of 12 interactive, inquiry-based biology simulations and exercises designed for college and AP high school biology students. Figure 7.5 shows sample screens from its *FlyLab.*

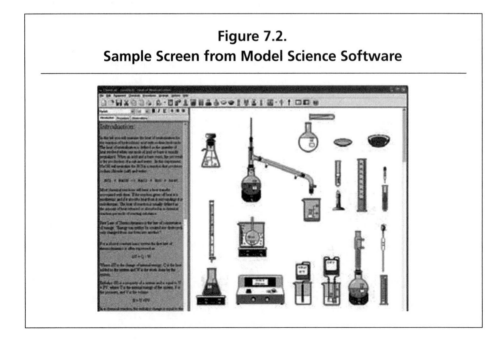

Figure 7.2.
Sample Screen from Model Science Software

Figure 7.3.
Acid Base Titration Experiment from VirtLab
(http://www.virtlab.com/index.aspx)

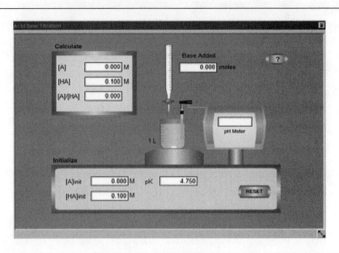

Figure 7.4.
Chemical Kinetics Experiment from Davidson
College's Virtual Chemistry Experiments
(http://www.chm.davidson.edu/vce/index.html)

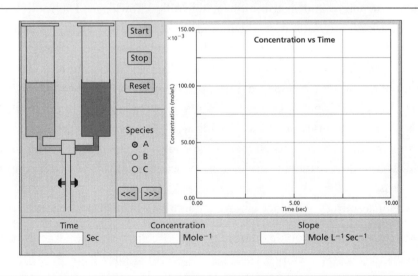

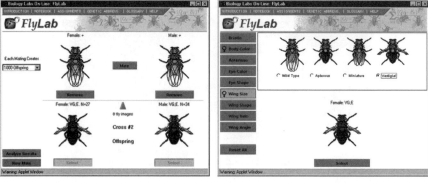

Figure 7.5.
Biology Labs On-line (http://www.biologylab.awlonline.com/)

Bioquest (http://bioquest.org/BQLibrary/library_result.php) is a free online library of biological graphics produced by a consortium of biology educators and course developers. They continue to develop this collection of realistic laboratory simulation software together with supplementary materials that reflect a research approach to learning. The written material that accompanies each module encourages students to think about the reasons behind their research design and implementation. It also stresses the social, historical, and philosophical sides of the construction and distribution of scientific knowledge. The modules are intended to shift attention from the mechanics of laboratory work, which is best learned by hands-on experience, to the why behind the student's strategic experimental plans and issues regarding persuasion through "publication."

Whitman College developed a *Virtual Pig* (www.whitman.edu/biology/vpd/main.html) dissection for biology students. It is not a true simulation, but instead contains a series of slides showing well-photographed views of various stages of the dissection process. Figure 7.6 shows an example. This site is also helpful as a guide for students performing dissections off campus with commercial lab kits.

Additional sources of science laboratory simulations include the following:

- *PhET* (http://phet.colorado.edu/index.php) A collection of interactive simulations in physics, chemistry, biology, and earth science from the University

Figure 7.6.
Virtual Pig Sample Slide

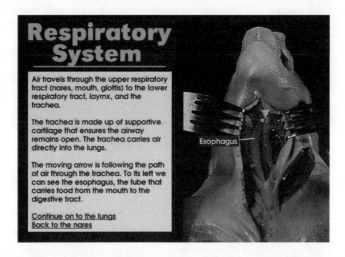

of Colorado at Boulder. However, most of their simulations are related to physics.

- *PhysicsLab* (www.physicslab.co.uk) A free collection of simulations from the United Kingdom.

- *PhysicsLessons.com iPhysics* (www.physicslessons.com/iphysics.htm) A free collection of physics simulations from PhysicsLessons.com and Explore Science.com.

- *The Virtual Physics Laboratory* (www.colpus.me.uk/vplabd) Sponsored by the National Physical Laboratory and the Institute of Physics of the United Kingdom, a commercial package that includes approximately 220 interactive experiments ranging from basic measurements to quantum physics.

- *Physlets* (http://webphysics.davidson.edu/Applets/Applets.html) These physics applets are small, flexible Java applets that can be used in a wide variety of online applications. Many of these have been developed by Davidson College, but many others are being produced around the world. Figure 7.7 shows a sample screen.

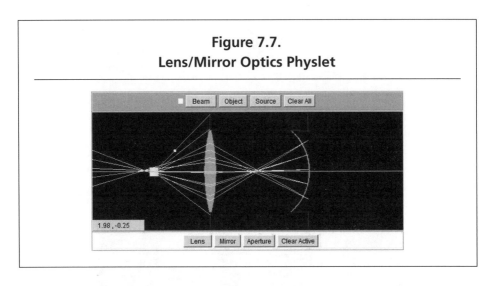

Figure 7.7.
Lens/Mirror Optics Physlet

Dr. Peter Jeschofnig has successfully used the lens/mirror optics bench simulation exercise shown in Figure 7.7 both in lieu of and as a pre-lab for a hands-on optical bench experiment with his online calculus-based physics courses. This excellent Java applet simulation was developed and made available for free by Wolfgang Christian and the *WebPhysics* staff at Davidson College in Davidson, South Carolina, and the exercise using the applet was created by Les Richardson of RichTech, Canada. Wolfgang Christian and Mario Belloni of Davidson College have also written an excellent text on how to incorporate physlets into a physics curriculum. The text, *Physlets: Teaching Physics with Interactive Curricular Material* (Christian and Belloni, 2001), also contains a CD with numerous readily usable simulations.

USING KITCHEN LABS AND INSTRUCTOR-ASSEMBLED KITS WITH ONLINE SCIENCE COURSES

As noted in Chapter 4, there are several kitchen science lab manuals, especially in chemistry, that can be effectively used to provide valid science laboratory experiences for introductory and non-science-majors' online courses. Because studies confirm that professional kitchen labs can provide students with successful learning opportunities, it can reasonably be assumed that kitchen labs created by creative online lab science instructors can be equally successful.

Incorporating experiments from kitchen science lab manuals or instructor-designed kitchen labs into a course curriculum is no different than incorporating experiments from traditional manuals. Instructors simply select the experiments that best match the learning objectives of their course content.

As with using commercial lab kits, instructors should perform all of the selected labs before the beginning of the semester to understand how they are performed so that they will be able to guide students through the procedures. The commercial kitchen lab manual should provide a list of supplies the students must procure, but where applicable the instructor should suggest specific brands of materials to promote consistency among student's results.

Although liability issues should not be a large concern with kitchen labs, instructors must still ensure their online students performing kitchen lab experiments receive standard laboratory safety instructions. It is also wise to have students provide a signed liability waiver in which they agree to follow all instructions and precautions and hold the institution and instructor harmless for any negative results of their experimentation activities.

If instructors create their own kitchen lab experiments, they should have a lab tech or colleague perform them to confirm their quality as a learning experience and to review the adequacy and correctness of the procedural directions and supply list. There is definitely a liability risk with instructor-created labs, so ample safety instructions and signed liability waivers are definitely needed.

Instructors who choose to design lab kits that are checked out or sold to students also need to ensure they provide adequate safety instructions and obtain liability waivers from students. The discussion about instructor-developed lab kits in Chapter 4 covers most of the things these instructors should consider. That section should be carefully reviewed by instructors considering this option so that they can think about how to mitigate potential problems and select the least troublesome way to supply, price, distribute, and account for the kit equipment and supplies they provide students.

To avoid safety, liability, and government regulation issues, instructors developing their own kits need to provide material safety data sheets (MSDSs) on all chemicals they give students to use at home. Current government prohibitions on distribution of chemicals should be checked to ensure that instructors are not in violation of any recent regulations. For example, although iodine has long been a seemingly innocuous stain commonly used in biology labs, its distribution in concentrations greater than 2.2% was recently prohibited by the U.S. government because it is used in the illegal production of methamphetamine.

Instructors designing their own kits should also try to employ microscale principles as much as possible and design their experiments to require the smallest quantities of chemicals and materials needed to produce a satisfactory reaction for students. This not only saves money and promotes safety, but it also simplifies disposal because microscale quantities can safely and legally be flushed down a sink and it makes compliance with governmental shipping regulations easier.

USING COMMERCIAL LAB KITS WITH ONLINE SCIENCE COURSES

An easy way to determine which experiments as well as the amount of lab work to assign for an online lab science course is to simply assign the same experiments that are performed in the campus version of the online course. Using the same labs is ideal because it equates the online with the on-campus learning experience and allows for comparative assessments and evaluations. This may not be feasible if very sophisticated science equipment or exceptionally hazardous organic chemistry supplies are used for the campus labs. However, commercial lab kits designed on the principles of small-scale chemistry can safely replicate for home use the vast majority of undergraduate science experiments conducted on campuses across the United States.

The same types of chemicals, even most hazardous ones, can be supplied in micro quantities by commercial lab kits. The equipment used may be modified for size, cost, and shipping concerns. In the titration example shown in Figure 7.8, despite modified and less expensive equipment, independent students have the same measurement, manipulation, and learning experiences as do on-campus students performing the same titration lab with a full-sized burette and stand.

Instructors can usually request a complementary copy of the manuals for standard commercially assembled lab kits and review them in advance to see which kits will best match their online-course needs. Commercially assembled lab kits for higher education should contain experiments aligned to the standard learning objectives traditionally associated with specific course disciplines. The kits tend to be textbook-agnostic and are likely to coincide nicely with existing campus labs and thus be perfect for use with online sections of the course. The lab kits normally include a lab manual plus all the science equipment, basic supplies, chemicals, and specimens a student needs to complete the experiments included in the kits' lab manuals.

Figure 7.8.
LabPaq Titration Experiment

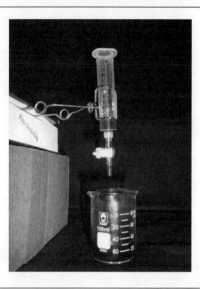

Microbiology kits include various nutrient agars and broths for growing cultures. Physics kits contain pulleys, centripetal force units, optical benches, resisters, multimeters, and other standard equipment. Kits for anatomy and physiology and science-majors biology courses that require dissections should include appropriately preserved specimens such as the fetal pig being dissected on a kitchen counter by a student in Figure 7.9.

Commercial lab kit suppliers also have lists of tested experiments that can be assembled into customized kits. Although it is possible to have a lab kit commercially customized, that usually assumes the annual course enrollments are at least a hundred or more and the institution is willing to make a multi-year commitment. Because small-batch kit customization and assembly is labor intensive, custom kits may cost more than standard kits even if they include fewer experiments. Whenever possible, utilizing standard kits is usually in the best economic interest of students and may, at no additional cost, include extra experiments for students who wish to perform optional credit work.

As noted earlier, relatively few companies are currently producing commercial lab kits containing experiments specifically aligned to the standard academic

Figure 7.9.
LabPaq Fetal Pig Dissection

curriculums of higher education. The oldest and largest of these is Hands-On Labs (HOL; www.LabPaq.com) in Englewood, Colorado, the authors' educator-owned company that has been designing, producing, and distributing LabPaq science lab kits since 1994. HOL produces LabPaqs in all science disciplines for college, allied health, and AP high school students. These include introductory, science-majors, and non-science-majors courses for biology, human anatomy and physiology, microbiology, nutrition, chemistry, physics, physical sciences, geology and earth sciences, environmental sciences, and forensics. HOL LabPaqs are primarily sold directly to students on a wholesale basis from its website and shipped within 24 hours of ordering.

Also located in Englewood, Colorado, eScience Labs (ESL; http://esciencelabs.com) began producing a limited but increasing number of commercially assembled lab kits in 2008. ESL produces a similar but more limited line of kits primarily designed for the middle and high school markets, but they are increasingly developing kits for college-level courses. ESL kits are sold through third party distributors as well as online.

Quality Science Labs (QSL; www.qualitysciencelabs.com) is a small, home-based company in Lake George, Colorado, that produces science lab kits for the middle and high school markets. However, they offer one AP high school chemistry kit that might also be used for first-year college courses. QSL kits are primarily sold online.

The issues an online instructor should consider in selecting a commercial lab kit supplier include the following:

- *Reliability and capacity of supplier:* Institutions and science educators devote a substantial amount of time and resources in the design of their online lab science courses. Instructors also invest considerable personal energies and time in organizing and/or reorganizing their course materials for online delivery as well as in familiarizing themselves with an adopted lab kit's structure and integrating its processes into their course. They normally expect these investments along with their basic course materials to have several years of useful life. Thus, the reliability and capacity of lab kit suppliers are paramount, because if suppliers cannot consistently produce and deliver quality lab kits to students, much of the institution's and instructors' investment in the course may be lost along with the institution's reputation and enrollment numbers.

- *Safety instructions and liability insurance:* It should be assumed that a lab kit made explicitly for off-campus and home use should be safe for adult college students. However, students will be students and ours is a litigious society. Despite layers of liability waivers and the questionable legitimacy of claims that may arise, no institution or instructor wants to be burdened by the time and expense required to defend a lawsuit. Thus, before adopting any specific lab kit, instructors should make sure that the kit's supplier carries ample liability insurance and that the supplier's policy will also indemnify them and their institution. This can be accomplished by requesting a certificate of insurance that lists the name of the instructor or instructors and the institution.

- *Reputation and customer service:* Before finalizing a lab kit adoption agreement, instructors should spend time talking with other adopters. It is important to learn of others' experiences with the specific lab kit and ensure the supplier's reliability for consistency and quality in their products as well as excellent customer services for students as well as instructors.

- *Quality experimental design:* For any lab kit under consideration, instructors should obtain a copy of the lab kit's manual and the kit's materials list. These materials should be carefully reviewed for quality of instructional design, alignment with course concepts, clarity of instructions, and an appropriate level of sophistication.

- *Quality packaging and materials:* Once an initial lab kit selection is made, an evaluation kit should be obtained so that the instructor can have firsthand knowledge of the quality and organization of its materials and packaging before the adoption is finalized. In light of the substantial cost of commercial lab kits and the potential for conflict of interest with institutional policies, evaluation kits are seldom supplied free of charge unless actually adopted. However, the price of evaluation lab kits is usually discounted for instructors. If an instructor's institution will not purchase an evaluation lab kit, some suppliers will loan one to the instructor to examine at no cost provided it is quickly returned in resalable condition.

How Commercially Assembled Lab Kits Are Ordered

In light of their tendency to contain unusual and potentially perishable supplies, higher education lab kits are not normally sold through bookstores and third parties but are instead shipped directly to students by the manufacturer in response to online orders. This also helps keep the costs down for students because no bookstore markup on the manufacturer's price is required. However, some institutions still prefer to have their adopted lab kits stocked by their bookstores. Thus, a science instructor should verify the exact purchase and distribution method that will be used because this will affect the price for students and possibly the lab kit's adoption agreement.

Like textbooks, commercially assembled lab kits are adopted by instructors and institutions but purchased by students. Once an instructor has adopted a lab kit, the lab kit's name and all specific ordering and purchasing details should be included in the course's online registration materials and syllabus. Unless the kits are being sold through the institution's bookstore, students typically go online to the manufacturer's website and directly order the lab kit for their course with a credit card. Financial aid officers normally set up accounts with the lab kit manufacturer and place orders in the name of financial aid students. These kits are directly shipped to the students and their bills sent to the financial aid office. Here is a sample syllabus notice advising students about their course's requirement for a lab kit.

> This course includes a laboratory component which you MUST complete by using commercially assembled lab kit #xx-xx. After you are certain you intend to take the course, order your lab kit directly online at www.XYZ.com. Financial aid students should contact their

financial aid advisor or campus bookstore for ordering instructions. It is important to keep your sales receipt and order number and be prepared to supply them to your instructor as proof of purchase of required course materials. Lab kits are normally shipped within one business day so it is not necessary to order them until you are certain you will take the course or a week before the first lab is assigned.

Manufacturers should ship lab kits to students within 24 hours of ordering so that the kits can be in students' hands within five working days. Thus, it is not necessary for students to order their kits far in advance. In fact, because there are usually substantial restocking fees plus tight restrictions and a narrow return window for lab kit returns, students should be encouraged to not order their kits until they are certain they intend to complete the course.

Students should be reminded and encouraged to immediately check all the contents of their lab kits upon arrival to ensure nothing is missing, broken, or malfunctioning. Most lab kit manufacturers are well aware that students may abuse and misplace things. For that reason, they will usually support a lab kit and unquestioningly correct any problems reported for only a short period of time after the lab kit is delivered. If a student waits until mid-semester to report something broken or missing, the manufacturer will assume the student is responsible for the problem and the student will have to pay for the replacement.

Commercial Lab Kit Adoption Process

Once an instructor has decided to use a commercial lab kit to cover the lab portion of his or her online course, the manufacturer needs to be notified and provided with semester start dates and approximate enrollment data per semester so that the kits can be scheduled for production. Lab kits have no use beyond higher education, often contain perishable items, and are usually produced only in response to institutions' needs. For these reasons, kit manufacturers normally require a formal adoption agreement with the instructor and the institution. These agreements actually protect the institution and instructor as well as the manufacturer because they minimize the institution's risk that it will not be able to conduct the online lab science course and the supplier's risk that its investment in labor and inventory will be wasted. Most adoption agreements can be cancelled with a six-month notice that allows both the institution and manufacturer to protect their interest.

Adoption agreements are primarily geared to ensure frequent communication between the manufacturer and the institution so that the manufacturer can match lab kit production to the estimated online science course enrollments. Procurement of lab kit contents can understandably be expensive and protracted for the manufacturer, especially for supplies that must be imported and for specially packaged and potentially perishable chemicals and biological specimens. Manufacturers want to ensure they procure adequate supplies to assemble appropriate quantities of lab kits for the instructor's students. Yet, they must also protect themselves from potential losses from over-procurement and over-producing kits that may not be purchased by students. It is in online science students' best interest that their instructor and institution work closely with their chosen lab kit manufacturer and keep it informed of any changes in enrollment as soon as they are known.

INCORPORATING LAB EXPERIMENTS AND LAB REPORTS INTO THE ONLINE COURSE

There are not many differences between on-campus and online courses when it comes to incorporating the lab experiments and lab reports into the course work. However, the few differences that do exist are substantial ones.

One of greatest advantages of adopting a commercially assembled lab kit for online science students to use off campus or at home is that instructors do not have to organize, manage, and supervise laboratory sessions. Instead they have more time to coach and to assist in and evaluate their students' learning experiences. However, the instructor will not be able to observe the students performing experiments, see the gleam of recognition in their eyes or the frown of confusion on their brows, observe how well or how poorly they are performing the procedures, or know if they are complying with all safety protocols. The only indication of students' activities and learning comes after the fact as the instructor reads the students' lab reports and postings to the lab discussion board.

This lack of direct supervision is not necessarily a bad thing, for it forces students to take responsibility for their own learning, and the result is usually a much deeper and more meaningful science discovery learning experience. However, the inability to supervise students' performance of lab work also means online science instructors must be as attentive and proactive as possible. They need to set the stage for students to get the most out of their experimental activities and should make students aware of the potential hazards and pitfalls in each experiment they are about to perform.

Biology professor Pamela Thineson of Century College made the following observation after her first semester of teaching an online biology class and using a commercially assembled lab kit:

> This has been a very successful class. I feel the students may have actually learned more in the online version than in my campus version, particularly for the labs because they had to do a lot of problem-solving without a teacher being right there to answer all their questions. Rather than e-mail me or put questions on the discussion board, many of them opted to "figure it out for themselves." And they *did* figure out much of it on their own or in collaboration with another student. I'm impressed by their hard work, perseverance and resourcefulness.

Safety is always paramount in experimentation, on campus as well as off campus. The lab kit's manual should contain an extensive safety section; if it does not, the instructor will have to create and deliver this information within the course content. To ensure that students have read and understood all laboratory safety instructions, it is recommended that instructors design a short quiz of randomly generated lab-safety questions. Students should be required to continue retaking different versions of the quiz until they achieve a grade of at least 90%.

Each lab module should introduce the experiment or experiments to be performed and tie the activities to related science concepts within the course content. The students should be required to read the experimental procedures a week in advance and to know what they will be doing and what materials they will need to organize before they begin to work. It is a good practice to have a short pre-lab quiz to encourage students to read and think about the experiment in advance of rushing into performing it. A simple pre-lab quiz might ask students to give a couple of hypotheses for the upcoming lab, to list potential hazards of the lab and how those hazards might be avoided, and to give their opinions about what results might be expected.

Although instructors will have performed most lab kit experiments at some point in their academic careers, it is a best practice for them to conduct all the lab kit's experiments and any assigned simulations in order to fully understand the procedures and to better coach students who run into problems. Where possible and needed, the instructor should give the students practical hints to facilitate their experimental activities, but without revealing expected results. These might include the following points:

- common mistakes students tend to make in performing the procedures
- approximately how much time is usually needed to observe a certain reaction
- how to best set up data tables for graphing and analysis
- potential results that may not be obvious or may be difficult to understand

Most importantly, instructors should try to provide information that helps make the experiment relevant to students' lives and also helps them relate the experimental results to the real world. To help keep students on track, instructors should frequently check lab discussion boards and respond to urgent lab questions and those that haven't been answered by other students within a few hours.

Grading formal lab reports for any type of laboratory experience can be extremely time-consuming. Thus, it is not surprising that many instructors resort instead to having students complete simple answer sheets about each experiment. However, the compiling of a formal lab report is an extremely important part of the multidisciplinary activities associated with learning science. It forces students to contemplate what they have done, to mathematically analyze data, to organize their thoughts, and to communicate their experimental activities in a clear and comprehensive manner. Plus it reinforces the processes of the scientific method and the importance of thoroughness and integrity in science work. The lab report allows students to unequivocally demonstrate that they performed an experiment and understood its implications.

Instructors should provide students with a copy of the grading rubric that will be used to assess formal lab reports. It is also helpful to post examples of excellent and poor lab reports, for when students know their instructor's expectations, they can better strive to meet them.

It is a science instructor's responsibility to thoroughly read and assess students' lab reports. However, there is a potentially acceptable alternative to always grading the students' formal lab reports covering every experiment performed during the semester. This option is especially applicable to introductory and non-science-major courses. After students have prepared a few lab reports, are clearly exhibiting evidence of performing and understanding their experiments, and have demonstrated that they genuinely understand the scientific method and know how a good lab report is written, then instructors might choose to substitute answer sheets or lab quizzes for as many as 50% of the remaining experiments. However, it is recommended that this not begin until after the second or third formal lab report.

Instructors should invest ample up-front time to assess their students' initial lab reports very, very critically—especially the very first one. Doing so sets the stage for high expectations and a rapid learning curve. Usually by the third formal lab report, students have been critiqued to the point that they fully understand and can deliver what is expected of them. The instructor can then be a hero, for the students will greatly appreciate not having to write formal reports for every one of the remaining labs. Instructors then have the luxury to assign formal lab reports for remaining experiments to coincide with their personal grading schedules or with labs that tend to be most difficult for students to comprehend.

Lab quizzes help reinforce what science students learned in their experimental activities. They can also provide evidence that students actually performed their labs, especially if the questions are ones that can be answered only by someone who actually performed the experiment. Instead of developing separate lab quizzes, questions related to the lab experiences can be easily incorporated into general course-content quizzes, assuming they are frequently given so instructors can quickly detect when students are possibly not performing their labs.

It is extremely important that science instructors quickly follow up on students who fall behind in submitting their lab reports or other lab assignments. Many students think they can perform all of their experiments during a marathon weekend of lab work once a month or at the end of the semester. This of course defeats the objective of relating experimental activities to course content. Also, the discussion board conversations will have less meaning to them. Rushing to complete lab assignments in a few marathon sessions instead of keeping current with the course and lab work is a recipe for probable failure as well as wasted laboratory science learning opportunities.

The Evidence Supporting Off-Campus Science Labs

The skepticism of early doubters who questioned the value and effectiveness of general online courses should be satisfied by the numerous and extensive studies that have increasingly refuted those doubts and well demonstrated the efficacy of online teaching. Whereas earlier studies indicated online instruction was "just as good as" and then "occasionally even better than," more recent quantitative studies unequivocally state that online instruction is "better than" face-to-face instruction (Allen & Seaman, 2008). But where's the evidence for online lab sciences courses and home-based science experimentation with lab kits? Can students really safely experiment off campus or at home and independently perform lab work assignments that will teach them what they really need to know?

As reflected in the following documented case studies, it actually is possible for students to safely perform rigorous, college-level science experimentation at home with commercial lab kits. As discussed in Chapters 4 and 7, these kits contain equipment, supplies, and detailed instructions to allow students to perform experiments that correlate to nationwide teaching objectives. The kits' lab manuals also describe, discuss, and reinforce conventional and home-lab safety concerns to help students to identify and deal with safety issues and to recognize these issues should they ever work in a formal laboratory facility. As with campus-based labs, most home lab kits require students to keep lab notes and submit formal lab reports for assessment. Their lab manuals usually include instructions about how to keep good lab notes and prepare formal lab reports as well as how to draw and label illustrations and prepare effective spreadsheets and graphs for data recording and analysis.

Online students must take more responsibility for their own learning because there is no instructor or lab assistant to organize the materials, set up the experiments, tell them what results to expect, and clean up after the lab. Thus, independent-use lab kits foster maturity and responsibility in online students.

Kathy Carrigan, an online chemistry professor at Portland Community College, finds that her online students using lab kits to experiment independently tend to more seriously contemplate the implications of their science laboratory experiences. Carrigan (to Hands-On Labs, personal communication, 2009) demonstrated this point by providing the following excerpt from a student's lab comments:

> At the beginning of this lab I thought that you'd simply put a couple of chemicals together and watch for a color change. Now after completing this lab I've learned that no matter what you expect to happen, it's not always the case. . . . I know that many chemical changes happen daily in nature, but I also know that we don't see most of them. I think after this experiment I will observe things differently. I know that when I mix my creamer in coffee I get a color change, but that's not all that important of a chemical change if any, or is it that the color change is due to the white mixing with the brown, I almost can't wait for morning now. . . . I do know that by mixing certain chemicals you can produce gases. A good example of this is that certain cleaners are toxic when mixed together. I think a simple observation I notice daily is the use of my tooth paste. When mixed with the moisture in your mouth it has a tendency to foam up. Not to mention if you use the tooth paste with baking soda. Too bitter and bubbly for me though.
>
> Chemical changes happen daily and like I said before are rarely noticed. I think one of the most overlooked is when the car takes off in front of you and you notice smoke, fumes and/or heat waves out of the exhaust. Little do people think of that chemical change

that is taking place inside the cars they drive. I do know that by burning something, it almost always goes into some form of chemical change. What I don't know is what is being produced by burning certain items.

The reason I ponder this, is because here in Iraq right now they burn all trash. They have a large burn pit that sits about 800 meters from where I live, work, eat and sleep. I just wonder what kinds of chemicals are being released into the air from all the chemical changes that are taking place. Right now I am more aware of chemical changes than I think most people are that live in the U.S. I just hope that these chemical changes are not dangerous, as I know so many can be.

ONLINE SCIENCE SUCCESS AT OCEAN COUNTY COLLEGE, TOMS RIVER, NJ

Ocean County College (OCC) was one of the first mid-Atlantic institutions to develop and place the majority of its lab science courses completely online. It did so by using lab kits to fulfill their courses' wet laboratory requirements. OCC's innovative, cost-effective, and environment-friendly online laboratory science courses have attracted students from across the country and around the world, have expanded OCC's enrollments in science programs, and have eliminated the need for the college to build an additional science laboratory building (Brown, 2009b).

The expansion in OCC's online science programs grew out of its award-winning One Day per Week Online/Web-Assisted Nursing Program. This unique program allows students to attend clinical training one day per week and receive the balance of their instruction online. Anatomy and physiology, microbiology, and chemistry are cornerstone courses in the prenursing curriculum: "The ability to effectively deliver these courses online ... has allowed OCC's nursing program to become a national model that attracts working individuals who otherwise could not pursue nursing studies" (Brown, 2009a).

OCC's online nursing program was initiated by Dr. James W. Brown, then the college's dean of Science, Engineering, Health Sciences, and Human Performance. Dr. Brown initially considered using virtual laboratory simulations for the program. Apart from their passive nature and questionable effectiveness as a substitute for wet labs, Dr. Brown rejected simulated labs primarily because many four-year colleges will not accept transfer science credits if they do not include hands-on laboratory experiences. Also, it was important to Dr. Brown that OCC students have authentic wet-laboratory experiences because he believes those experiences are "vital to honing critical thinking skills via the trials and errors manifested in laboratory practices" (Brown, 2009a).

Dr. Brown accredits science lab kits with providing OCC the ability to take its award-winning nursing program completely online and thus assist in its mission to help eliminate America's nursing shortage. OCC surveys confirmed that nursing students found their online courses to be a convenient and popular way to learn, and assessments of online and F2F students' learning were favorably comparable. Further, student responses were overwhelmingly positive. Today, increasing numbers of students from other countries as well as other states register for OCC's online nursing program.

The success of the anatomy and physiology, microbiology, and chemistry courses within the online nursing program led OCC to develop additional online science courses in chemistry, biology, and physics for their traditional degree programs. Today OCC offers 14 different science courses and an entire associate of science degree program completely online by using commercial lab kits for the laboratory component. According to Dr. Brown and his colleagues, this has been a tremendous success and alleviated pressure to build another facility to keep up with laboratory science course demand (Brown et al., 2009). This success is evidenced by Dr. Brown's graph (Figure 8.1) reflecting OCC's growth in totally online science courses for the academic years 2005, 2006, and 2007. See the Appendix of this book for a detailed case study by Dr. Brown describing his experiences in bringing the microbiology course fully online at OCC.

These positive assessments are complemented by the following student feedback quotes by provided by OCC anatomy and physiology professor Marc LaBella (as cited in Brown et al., 2009):

- "I couldn't be happier that I switched to the online section of the course."
- "The online labs actually work! I learned so much more than I would have in a face-to-face laboratory. They were fun and you enjoy learning."
- "It allows me to be a full-time mom and knock off my nursing prerequisites at the same time."
- "My nursing school in Alaska told me that I couldn't take A & P until September. So I decided to take it now in New Jersey."

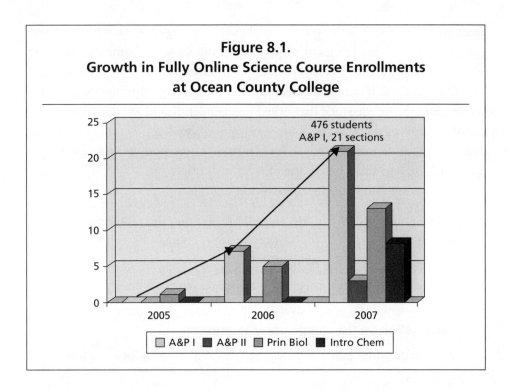

Figure 8.1.
Growth in Fully Online Science Course Enrollments at Ocean County College

476 students
A&P I, 21 sections

A&P I   A&P II   Prin Biol   Intro Chem

A feedback comment with even more weight regarding the effectiveness of online lab science and home-based lab kits comes from OCC's professor Dr. Marsha Bradley (2008):

> I had been teaching A & P for over 20 years and never thought it should be taught online. My colleague showed me the positive results from his online A & P course using LabPaqs. Now that I have been teaching the course online for several years, I am one of the converts who say yes, you can really teach A & P online with a genuine hands-on experience.

ONLINE SCIENCE SUCCESS AT COLORADO MOUNTAIN COLLEGE

In the fall of 2006, Dr. Peter Jeschofnig conducted a quantitative study comparing assessment results between his F2F and online Chemistry 111 courses at Colorado Mountain College (Jeschofnig, 2006). He first had all students take a proctored exam produced by the American Chemical Society. Both groups were given the same assignments, quizzes, and exams throughout the semester. Both groups used the same lab manual, performed the same experiments, and were required to write formal lab reports that were graded with the same rubric. The only difference was that the campus students worked in groups in a campus laboratory, and the online students worked independently and at home using a lab kit. At the end of the semester, both groups again took a proctored exam produced by the American Chemical Society. In addition, both groups also took a final exam Dr. Jeschofnig had written for his institution.

Dr. Jeschofnig's study made the following findings:

- F2F and online scores for the national American Chemical Society (ACS) exams both pre- and post-course were basically equivalent, with a mean score of 40.4 for F2F and 40.9 for online.

- F2F and online instructor-prepared exam scores were also basically equivalent.

- Online students' lab grades averaged 5% higher and online course grades averaged 1% higher than the grades of F2F students.

- Instructor-prepared exams were as effective as ACS exams for assessment.

- Conclusions:

  - Student learning in online Chemistry 111 courses with home-based lab kits is at least equivalent to and usually a bit better than in F2F courses with a campus-based lab.

  - Valid Chemistry 111 assessment can be achieved via instructor-created exams.

The following semester Dr. Jeschofnig conducted a similar comparative study of his campus-based and online Chemistry 112 courses. The comparative results for Chemistry 112 were almost identical to those for Chemistry 111, and the conclusions of the study were the same.

ONLINE SCIENCE SUCCESS AT HERKIMER COUNTY COMMUNITY COLLEGE, NY

Jennifer Herzog, an assistant professor of biology for Herkimer County Community College, part of the SUNY system, has been conducting similar studies comparing grade results between her on-campus (F2F) and online courses since 2001 (Herzog, 2008). Cumulative averages reflect that her online courses have a substantially higher drop-out rate than F2F courses (35% versus 11% for F2F);

however, this difference appears to be decreasing as assessments to gauge students' capacity for online coursework have matured to weed out students who erroneously think online courses are a cakewalk. The most striking difference to Herzog is between her online and on-campus students' final grades. Her online students' grade averages are almost 12 points higher than her campus-based students (82.5 versus 75.8 for F2F), and 62% of her online students earn an A or B in the course versus only 43% of F2F students. Herzog (2008) states:

> Overall, I am very happy I took on the challenge of developing an Internet-based college biology lab course. It has been a lot of work (and continues to be!) but the rewards have been well worth the effort. I truthfully never thought that this course would even get off the ground for a multitude of reasons. However, my interactions with my students have made me realize that teaching a lab science in this venue can be done successfully, . . . and moreover can be fun!

Online Teaching Advice from the Pros

As science instructors gain experience and confidence in teaching their disciplines online, they are learning the strategies that work best in organizing their course and in helping their students correctly perform their lab assignments and gain meaning from the online course content. To assist in this process, we asked distinguished and well-seasoned online science educators from a variety of disciplines to share their thoughts about how teaching science online is different from teaching other subjects and from teaching face-to-face, to describe the tools they find most effective, to discuss how they integrate lab experiences into their courses, and to consider what advice they would give to new online instructors. The following represents a summary of their comments.

ANATOMY AND PHYSIOLOGY PROFESSOR DR. LASZLO VASS

Dr. Laszlo Vass has been teaching general biology as well as anatomy and physiology online for CCCOnline and the Community College of Denver for over seven years. He also teaches biology and anatomy and physiology at Monarch High School in Louisville, Colorado, and serves on the Colorado State Science Commission. Vass (2007) offers these observations and suggestions.

- Science classes integrate theory into practice:

   No matter if it's a kindergartner exploring the wonders of dry ice or an undergraduate student participating in genetic research, theory and practice always go together . . . and unlike most other subjects, you don't have to know a lot of theory to observe and ask questions about natural phenomena.

- To teach science online, the instructor has to be "very organized, have a vision for the class as a whole, and be an excellent communicator."

- The discussion board is an online course's most important tool. But Vass also takes advantage of the advances in technology and uses student videos, animations, and podcast and vodcasting of lectures and dissections. He reports receiving "overwhelmingly positive responses for my efforts."

- Vass uses lab kits with his online courses and chooses the activities after reviewing the course's scope and sequence and doing all of the labs himself. He tries to anticipate where students may have difficulty and develop plans to prevent these problems.

- "My best advice to a new online science educator," says Vass, "is to try to think like a student" as he or she develops the course. He also recommends asking for help setting up the course from the "growing community of online instructors and lab kit vendors." He counsels:

   Be patient. It will take a semester or two to find your groove. If something doesn't work out, don't panic; assure your students that you are there for them and you can work with them to correct the situation. Have fun. Experiment and try new things. If they don't work, chalk it up to 'science' and try something else. Lastly, make your self available to your students. . . . Open, prompt communication is the single most important factor to running a successful online course.

CHEMISTRY PROFESSORS DR. PAUL VORNDAM AND DR. PETER JESCHOFNIG

Dr. Paul Vorndam, CCCOnline Science Department chair and former department chair for CSU-Pueblo, and Dr. Peter Jeschofnig, professor emeritus and prior Science Department chair of Colorado Mountain College, have both taught chemistry online and at a distance for over a decade. They contend the biggest difference in teaching science versus other subjects is that science focuses on problem solving, so an online science instructor must become adapt at walking students through problem-solving processes from a distance. In August 2009 conversations with Linda Jeschofnig, they proffered the following suggestions:

- To get students thinking about lab safety before beginning lab work, start the lab discussion board with questions regarding lab safety: What lab safety rules do you think students usually follow? Seldom follow? Which will be the hardest for you to follow and why?

- If using a lab kit, remind students to verify that their kit contains all of its listed supplies, that no items were damaged in transit, and that all electronics are functioning. Once an experiment has been started, it is frustrating to have to wait for replacement parts. Also the suppliers may have a limited time during which replacements can be obtained free of charge.

- Remind students to immediately check their lab manual and simulation CDs to ensure they work on their system. They shouldn't wait until they start their lab work to find out if they have a problem.

- If students carefully pre-read each experiment's procedures, they are less likely to waste the limited amount of chemicals in the lab kit. Because federal regulations allow only small amounts of chemicals to be shipped, lab kits usually contain only enough chemicals to perform an experiment once or twice.

- Before students begin a new experiment, start a discussion board brainstorming session to explore potential hypotheses. This gives students who are weaker in forming hypotheses a good starting point for the scientific method.

- When using lab kits, the instructor should perform each experiment beforehand to learn its potential pitfalls and then point them out to the students via the discussion board.

- Students often need instructions on how to carefully observe reactions that are faint and not immediately obvious. For example, when students are reacting potassium iodine solution with a 1% sodium hypochlorite solution, most of them see the vivid iodine-colored center, but few observe the weakly visible pink outer ring. And some students actually miss the formation of gas bubbles when sodium bicarbonate is reacted with hydrochloric acid. It improves a reaction's visibility for most students if they place black or white paper under their reaction's plates.

- Encouraging students to share their experimental data after all lab reports have been submitted gives them access to a greater volume of data for statistical treatment, comparison, analysis, and further discussion.

- Graphing skills are important for displaying the results of observations. Most students are familiar with Excel and similar spreadsheet programs, but very few know how to convert tables of their experimental data into an x-y graph or how to have the spreadsheet calculate the slope of the line. Help them by assigning an Excel tutorial online. Tutorials may also be included in their lab manual.

- Point out to students who do not have access to MS Office software that Open Office software is available via a free download from the Internet and will work as well.

- It buttresses learning and breaks the monotony of weekly lab reports and quizzes to occasionally let students select their own assessment activity to demonstrate they performed and learned from their lab assignment. They might write and act out a rap song summarizing the theory their lab work confirmed or produce a video summary of their experiment. Allowing students to combine their creativity with their lab experiences increases their enthusiasm for science. In this age of social media, students often proudly post these science lab projects on their Facebook page or on YouTube.

MICROBIOLOGY AND A & P PROFESSOR DR. CINDY JONES

In addition to teaching microbiology online for CCCOnline, Dr. Cindy Jones also teaches online human anatomy and physiology and phytochemistry, owns an herb and botanicals farm in northern Colorado that produces numerous aromatic and medicinal herbal products (www.sagescript.com), is a distinguished medical writer who has written several books and articles for natural health publications, serves as a research consultant to several health and medical organizations, and is a frequent guest on radio and television programs.

- Jones (L. Jeschofnig, personal communication, September 22, 2009) believes teaching science is substantially different from teaching other subjects because "it requires more extensive background knowledge and understanding than learning other subjects . . . [and] it is interrelated to every aspect of life." She adds that science requires observation and verification, and it teaches logic as well as subject matter.

- She says that the primary difference between teaching science online and in a classroom is that students cannot ask questions online and get immediate answers. Consequently, online students need to be independent and motivated, and online instructors need to be responsive and able to communicate well in writing. In her view, online discussions are the most important learning and teaching tool for online science courses, and "it is the instructors' responsibility to ensure that discussions are stimulating, relevant, and remain focused on course topics." She advocates discussion board participation to ensure that students keep up with the course and to enable students who tend to be quiet in classrooms to share their understandings.

- Jones likes lab kits because they provide hands-on learning experience for every student. In addition, with lab kits it is possible to make multi-day observations, which can't be done during standard lab sessions.

- Because lab kits and other course materials are expensive, it's important to let potential students know the approximate costs before they sign up for the class. "The total cost of an online course can be a financial strain on students," says Jones, "and should never come as a surprise to them. However, financial aid will cover the cost of lab kits just as it will textbooks."

- Online microbiology students need to fully learn sterile technique. Jones supplements the lab kit's manual with her lecture notes and website references. She also gives a quiz or has students write a paper on sterile techniques (as well as lab safety) before they grow their first colony, which helps her correct any misunderstandings early in the course.

- A challenge for online microbiology instructors is knowing whether students have really grown any bacteria, whether it is the correct bacteria, or whether they have contaminated their plates with something unrelated. To compensate for this potential problem, Jones has her students include photos of their cultures in their lab reports as well as verbal descriptions of the bacterial colonies they observe on their plates. She also directs students to websites with pictures of correctly grown cultures for comparison.

- An active and stimulating discussion board is very important to online microbiology courses. Jones reports, "My online students often comment that they learn as much, if not more, about microbiology from participation in the course discussion boards than from reading the text." To involve students in the discussion board, instructors need to continually provide thought-provoking questions, relevant websites and online resources, current references, and links to photos, illustrations, video clips, and other graphic aids. Jones adds that "textbook publishers usually offer an extensive library of excellent graphic learning objects that instructors can incorporate into their content materials and link to discussion topics."

PHYSICS PROFESSOR RUSTY ROE

CCCOnline online physics professor Rusty Roe is an astrophysicist who worked on NASA's Apollo 11 and 12 lunar landing programs and taught for the Air Force Academy. He believes the most important task of online science instructors is to convey a picture of the physical world to their students. They must be well equipped with excellent verbal, mathematical, and visual tools to communicate course materials and to respond to questions in a manner that provides three-dimensional clarity for their students. They must speak the language of mathematics clearly and be able to use graphs and images in ways that convey understanding and a physical interpretation of space-time (L. Jeschofnig, personal communication, January 2010). Roe feels these elements are vital to an effective online science course:

- A course schedule that identifies all required assignments and experiments by due date
- A lab report rubric that clearly explains the course diagnostics for students
- Equation editor tools that are intuitive for students to use
- Chat-collaboration tools that allow students to exchange explanations and understanding between themselves and their instructor
- A good lab kit with experiments that communicate the analytical-to-empirical meaning of the subject matter and allow students to see firsthand how the physical world responds to stimulus
- A lab manual that clearly explains all procedural steps and sets the stage for the experiment and empirical results expected
- Instructors should be proactive in pointing out potential problem areas where students often encounter difficulties. For example, physics students working

with electric circuits often set their digital multimeters incorrectly and blow the fuse. They are less likely to do this if their instructor gives them prior warning via the lab discussion board.

BIOLOGY PROFESSOR KATE LORMAND

Kate Lormand has been a college biology educator for 25 years and has taught online for 7 years. She states, "At first I was rather skeptical of how effective teaching and learning science online would be. I have overall been pleasantly surprised at how well it actually works for students. I doubt that the online format will ever completely replace traditional face-to-face education, but it can and does well meet the needs of many students" (L. Jeschofnig, personal communication, November 4, 2009). Her list of best practices includes the following:

- *Be wary of sarcasm in e-mails and online correspondence.* Students may not always discern the instructor's tone (or vice-versa), so always identify a tongue-in-cheek statements with a parenthetical "(ha-ha!)" or a happy face (☺).

- *Answer e-mails promptly and in a positive tone.* Lormand has found that many online students feel insecure, especially at the beginning of the term. She advises reassuring them that they are performing as expected and being patient and taking the time to "kindly explain and re-explain things to them, even things contained in the syllabus."

- *Understand that computers sometimes do eat exams.* Lormand recommends being flexible and willing to compromise because "most online students are very dedicated and responsible individuals who are serious about their education."

- *Laboratory experiments for online science classes are usually conducted in students' kitchens.* The instructor should remind students to clean their work area before and after each experiment "to avoid contaminating their work as well as their family (☺)," notes Lormand.

- *Before the first lab activity, send an e-mail to all students.* They need to know how home experiments differ from on-campus labs: They may take longer, especially at first, and each student must fill the role of the laboratory technician who prepares the lab, the student who performs the experiment, and the clean-up crew who puts everything safely away. However, by playing all these roles, students will genuinely grasp the concepts of the experiment.

- *Online instructors are actually coaches,* although they can feel they are simply "cyber-shuffling managers." Their discussion boards become the classroom where interaction helps the students "understand science concepts, become critical thinkers, and explore their own ideas about science." Discussion topics should be relevant both to the subject matter and to the real world. Lormand says, "Helping students to make these connections will help them to enjoy learning and become life-long learners."

- *The syllabus needs to be very easy to read, somewhat repetitive, and very clear.* Lormand recommends bold topic headings and bulleted points for important information. She says, "Students want to know exactly (1) what is due, (2) when it is due, (3) how it should be done, and (4) how many points it is worth. That information should be prominent and easy to find."

Lormand concludes:

> Overall, being an online science educator has been a very rewarding experience. You can and do make meaningful connections with the students. In many ways I've found online students are harder working and more dedicated than traditional students despite the fact that many have full-time jobs. I have found my online students genuinely care about what they are learning and they take their studies very seriously. They do their own work and seldom cheat. I have had only two online cheaters in two years, but have had several times that many cheaters in my face-to-face classes! Flexibility and understanding are the keys to being a successful online science educator. Oh, and it helps if you really care about students.

GEOLOGY PROFESSOR TRINA RIEGEL

Trina Riegel has been teaching online physical geology and historical geology courses since 2000 and has taught for CCCOnline, Laramie County Community College, Pikes Peak Community College, and the University of Maryland. In 2005 and 2006 Riegel put some real distance into distance education by teaching her courses from northern Italy and writing a blog for her students about the geologic sites she visited and researched. She thrives on the excitement of learning via first-hand observations and loves to recount her exciting geologic adventures. A favorite is about how, as a graduate student studying layers of clay minerals spanning millions of millenniums around Lake Michigan, she discovered and had a "Eureka!" grasp of how Lake Michigan had been both smaller and larger than it is today. This explains why she believes field trips are an important element in any geology course, even one online (L. Jeschofnig, personal communication, November 11, 2009). She believes science is the search for truth through experimentation and direct observation and that learning science differs from learning other subjects because it involves more active participation and relies on observational skills. She makes these observations about teaching geology online.

- The advantage of an online geology class is that geology is all around and easy to observe; students can see geological phenomena wherever they live. The biggest challenge is the lack of physicality; she can't pass around a fascinating crystal for students to observe. However, she's learned how to instead convey the beauty and shape of a crystal via graphics found online.

- Riegel finds online teaching more effective than on-campus courses "because it forces students to participate and includes those who won't speak up in class. Online students voice their observations, take preliminary steps toward interpretation, and discuss multiple working hypotheses." She finds threaded discussions about the results of experiments and field trips and suggesting future studies are the most successful for this purpose.

- Her students perform active geologic labs with their kits, and they also take a self-directed field trip. She has them research, find, and visit nearby outcrops so that they can see the rocks and minerals in nature that they are studying in the course and practice their identification skills as well. She reports that "the hands-on labs and field trip assure that credits for my course are transferable to other colleges and give my students 'core competencies.'"

- She defines three core competencies achieved by the lab activities: (1) critical thinking, which is developed by having to complete lab assignments on one's own; (2) collaboration through online discussion boards, "where students seek help, exchange procedural tips, share findings, and explore implications from the outcomes of their experimental activities"; and (3) communication in the form of detailed lab notes and a summary of lab experiences and findings in a formal lab report.

- In Riegel's words, online science instructors should "try to convey the sense of wonder and enthusiasm inherent in the love and understanding of science."

BIOLOGY PROFESSOR MARGE VORNDAM

Marge Vorndam, instructor, course designer, and co-chair of the Science Department at CCCOnline, has taught online biology for science majors, environmental science, and botany for almost a decade. She has been employed in the field of biology for over 35 years, working for the U.S. Fish and Wildlife Service, the U.S. Army Corps of Engineers, the U.S. Natural Resources and Conservation Service, other government agencies, in private industry R&D, and in environmental engineering. She shared her observations about teaching science online in an interview conducted by Linda Jeschofnig (August 29, 2009).

- Vorndam believes teaching science is different from teaching other academic disciplines. "Because science is based on research and on facts that have been quantified or proven, its content is approached differently than in other subjects. There are few subjective elements in science. Its judgments are objectively drawn from direct observations and accumulated quantitative data."

- She also emphasizes that the tools required to learn science are different from those used in liberal arts courses. Science understanding necessitates personal exploration, and elements of risk are associated with using the exploratory technology needed to acquire and verify science information.

- She also asserts that associating students' learning styles to course design is more critical in science than in liberal arts courses because the way people come to life dictates how they will perform research and in the subfields of science toward which they might gravitate.

- The online instructor's primary role is to continuously engage and re-engage students. This helps students to become invested in their learning, to engage in stimulating discussions that enhance their interest in and knowledge of the subject, and to analyze their own responses and think critically. Discussion boards also help instructors to see students' issues, perspectives, and errors and can provide new information and knowledge to instructors too. It is important to make students aware this is a mutual learning relationship and encourage them to teach their teacher.

- Vorndam feels it is imperative that instructors not let their online students fall behind in their coursework. Students must be encouraged to invest themselves in the course work. Usually reminding them of future employment benefits and relating their coursework to the achievement of their ultimate goals will help turn around errant and absent students.

- Although simulations are useful for illustrating concepts, Vorndam believes online students must have opportunities to perform hands-on experiments. Lab work helps to illuminate the points students are studying in their text, to provide them with applications of their course materials to real life, and to create deeper levels of science understanding. Like balancing a checkbook, science is a process that requires pragmatic steps, math calculation skills, and exactness to generate appropriate results.

- Teaching a science course online takes more of instructors' time. However, instructors can work at a time and place convenient to them. Just like their students, instructors also enjoy the ease and flexibility online courses provide as well as the financial and time savings realized from not commuting to campus.

The Tipping Point for Online Science Is Now!

A major tipping point toward online courses as the primary instructional mode of the future has been reached. Over 4 million higher education students are taking online courses as this book is being written (Means, Toyama, Murphy, Bakla, & Jones, 2009). Online enrollments are growing at over four times the pace of on-campus enrollments and this trend is expected to continue for at least another decade (Jaschik, 2009). "Responding to rising demand" was cited as the top issue confronting online education over the next two to three years by administrators (Green, 2009).

Still, relatively few institutions and instructors are offering their lab science courses and programs in a fully online format, and this must change. That same tipping point reached by online education in general is also pointing toward a future of increasing demand for online lab science courses. Students want fully online lab science courses. Society needs fully online lab science courses. And it is possible to effectively teach lab science courses fully online.

The examples in this book show that lab science courses can be successfully taught 100% online. They also affirm that college and even high school students can safely and independently learn important science concepts via home-based science experimentation. There is no longer any reason for institutions and instructors to hesitate. The continuing and escalating growth in online education will not abate anytime soon. Online instruction will increasingly become a primary mode of instruction (Allen & Seaman, 2008), so laboratory science courses must be taught in this mode.

Science education is now at that proverbial fork in the road. Will science instructors and institutions of higher education bravely and deliberately embrace 21st-century instructional delivery methods and distribute science knowledge in ways that meet the needs of today's online students? Will laboratory science courses begin to be increasingly taught online; or will they increasingly fall farther behind in the online world? Will U.S. students have the opportunity to satisfy the science requirements for their degree programs and to pursue science-related careers at places and times of their own choosing or necessity, or will the United States continue to decline into a state of science ignorance in a world of cyber-learning?

Skeptics initially doubted that online courses could ever be as effective as face-to-face (F2F) instruction. Over the decade since online education's inception, increasing evidence has shown that online courses "could be as effective" as, then that they "were as effective" as, and finally that they are "actually more effective" than F2F courses (Means et al., 2009). The Sloan Foundation's report *Staying the Course: Online Education in the United States, 2008* (Allen and Seaman, 2008) unequivocally refutes skeptics' biases against online courses.

There has been a similar progression of disbelief and then mounting evidence of success about online lab science courses. As previously discussed, the increasing numbers of anecdotal stories, supporting surveys, and quantitative studies accumulated by Hands-On Labs (2009) over the past decade have confirmed for us and for other educators the effectiveness of home-based experimentation with commercial science lab kits and shown that online science students using them usually perform better, have more satisfying learning experiences, and make higher grades than their campus-based peers.

The reasons for the success of online lab sciences courses and home-based science experimentation appear self-evident. Students must invest more time and active engagement in online coursework as well as in performing lab work independently, and they face no time constraints to thoroughly explore scientific concepts and enjoy discovery learning experiences. Further, the tactile nature of home-based science experimentation creates powerful and personally meaningful learning experiences. These discovery-learning processes are undoubtedly more difficult and time-consuming, but as confirmed in the Learning Pyramid, such higher-level learning processes generate higher levels of understanding and engender greater levels of personal pride and self-satisfaction. Because students own their self-found knowledge in fully online lab science courses, their higher levels of learning are not surprising. Such fantastic learning opportunities should be encouraged.

If science educators' institutions are not pushing them, then science educators should be pushing their institutions to offer lab science courses and programs fully online. Not only will this provide valid science learning experiences that satisfy the needs of today's busy mobile students, it will also help ensure and expand their institutions' enrollments and protect their livelihoods.

Sadly, 48% of the institutions with online programs surveyed by the Western Cooperative for Educational Telecommunications (WCET) and the Campus Computing Project did not know if their programs were profitable (Green, 2009). However, over 90% of the 52% of institutions that had studied this issue found their online courses were indeed profitable, and 54% of these reported profits greater than 15% (Green, 2009). Potential financial infusions from online programs could go a long way toward ensuring an institution's sustainability and the security of its science instructors' positions, especially during these difficult economic times.

Educational institutions must survive and prosper if they are to educate students and retain staff. This point alone should sway reluctant science instructors to encourage their institutions to offer fully online science courses. Further, those who make the effort to educate themselves as online lab science instructors and to structure their courses for fully online delivery will also enhance their personal potential. Not only will they foster the financial health of their institutions while improving science accessibility for online students, they will also become more valuable to other institutions as well as to their own and thus improve their future employment possibilities.

Educator advocates of online science should enlist the support of colleagues and present their administration with united proposals to plan, develop, and launch fully online lab science courses and programs. Even skeptics can be persuaded to lend support to this cause if they are helped to understand how online science instruction is vital to the growth and sustainability of their institutions and how the availability of online lab science courses can actually strengthen their potential to teach in a traditional face-to-face manner should they choose not to teach online. After all, even though demand for online courses is growing, a continuing need for F2F instruction will not disappear, especially not at vibrant and successful institutions.

Most institutions already use a learning management system (LMS) for content delivery and management or at least partial support of their campus-based courses. It should not be a huge leap for LMS-savvy F2F science instructors to convert the balance of their content and their LMS skills to the service of online students. Before fully moving their science course online, those skeptical of home labs might begin by allowing a test group of F2F students to utilize home-based lab kits and then compare their work to that of campus lab students to evaluate the lab kits' effectiveness.

Administrators who recognize the imperative of moving lab science courses online and are serious about doing so should communicate ample encouragement and provide ample support to willing faculty. If there are no willing faculty, administrations should protect the future of their institutions by specifically recruiting and hiring some. However, existing faculty should first be made aware of that necessity and given the opportunity to volunteer for such appointments before new faculty is hired. Administrators must then allocate adequate time and resources for faculty training, for instructional design and course development, and for technical support. They should quickly identify and assemble the resources online science faculty will require to rapidly move their lab science courses online and actualize the courses as soon as possible.

Where possible, practicing online instructors, even those from other disciplines, should be solicited as mentors for new online science faculty. Despite potentially different disciplines, there are many areas of instructional overlap, and personal mentors can greatly minimize new online instructors' learning curves, especially with new technology and demonstrating how it can be used to enhance instruction. There are ample existing and emerging resources available to quickly train instructors and move courses online; most are just a Google search or professional peer referral away. Institutions that utilize these resources and rapidly deploy their lab science courses online are more likely to retain and grow their enrollments than those who hesitate and come late to the party.

There is a valid sense of urgency by instructors, institutions, and society for quickly moving lab science courses online. They all have a vested interest in the numerous online students who need to quickly fulfill their degree requirements, to quickly bring their studies to a close, to quickly obtain jobs in health and science fields, to quickly improve the life of their families, and to quickly bolster the economy of their communities. Daily headlines reflect the impending perils to a world lacking science literacy and well-honed problem-solving skills.

The myriad of science and nonscience issues immediately facing today's complex world requires its students, its future workers, and its voters to quickly obtain a solid understanding of the processes of nature that science illuminates and to develop the exceptional problem-solving and decision-making skills needed to better address global problems.

The bias against online lab science courses that could quickly provide broader access to science education and problem-solving skills to home-based students has been proven groundless. Tested instructional elements are already in place to deliver effective lab science course fully online. With the barriers to online science broken and in light of the pressing need for expanded science education, lab science educators and academic institutions must quickly begin to move online, provide a full spectrum of online lab science courses for their students, and spur science learning forward through fully online lab science instruction.

APPENDIX
A CASE STUDY FROM START TO FINISH: THE WHY AND HOW OF PLACING MICROBIOLOGY COMPLETELY ONLINE AT OCEAN COUNTY COLLEGE

Dr. James Brown

This example was contributed by Dr. James Brown of Ocean County College to illustrate both the administrative and instructional thought and action processes related to why the college moved sections of their microbiology and other lab science courses from campus to 100% online course delivery. We felt it would be helpful to science instructors to directly learn what a renowned and distinguished science educator believes to be the best and most successful practices in teaching a lab science course online. Many instructors think that of all the lab science disciplines, microbiology is possibly the most difficult for instructors to teach and for students

About the chapter author: Dr. James W. Brown is currently an associate professor of science at Ocean County College teaching microbiology, biology, introduction to public health, and contemporary health. He is the former dean of Science, Engineering, Health Sciences and Human Performance at OCC. While he was dean, 14 totally online courses in the sciences were developed and are now offered completely online, making Ocean County College one of the first community colleges on the East Coast to accomplish such a feat.

to learn in a fully online format. However, Dr. Brown's practices and experiences clearly refute such a belief.

THE ADMINISTRATIVE CHALLENGES

Ocean County College (OCC), a mid-sized community college serving over 14,000 students on the New Jersey Shore, was running out of space in their brand-new Hiering Science Building, which had just opened in 2002. This growth was fueled by a highly successful one day per week (ODPW) nursing program that allowed nursing students to pursue an associate degree nursing program while spending just one day per week on campus to complete their clinical training. The balance of their didactic training was obtained online.

This ODPW program allowed OCC to increase its admittance of nursing program students from 150 to 240 per year. It also allowed access into a nursing program to a population of students not previously served due to family, job, or distance constrictions. The program was supported by a $458,000 New Jersey Health Initiatives Grant sponsored by the Robert Wood Johnson Foundation (Kearns et al., 2006).

Almost immediately, it became apparent that the prerequisite courses for the nursing program needed to be completely online as well. What good is a one day per week nursing program if the students must also spend three days a week on campus for their human anatomy and physiology I and II or microbiology classes? General education–required courses such as mathematics and humanities, English I and II, general psychology and contemporary health, and so on were already online. A & P I and II and microbiology needed to be placed fully online so that prenursing students could take these prerequisite courses before entering the demanding nursing curriculum. A & P I and II and microbiology were the stumbling block to the future success of the ODPW nursing program.

RUNNING OUT OF SPACE IN THE SCIENCE BUILDING

The dean of science and engineering had just retired. I had been approached to consider expanding my role as the dean overseeing nursing, allied health, and health and human performance to include the areas of science and engineering as well. My educational background was in microbiology; I had an extensive background in putting courses totally online; and we had just finished the first three years of the ODPW nursing program, so it would be a good fit for me. My new title, dean of Science, Engineering, Health Sciences and Human Performance, would encompass about one third of the academic portion of the college. The major focus would be to place science courses totally online and help to alleviate the pressure on the new Hiering Science Building, which was rapidly running out of laboratory space. Lab science classes in the Hiering Science Building were running Monday through Friday from 8 a.m. to 11 p.m. and Saturdays from 8 a.m. to 5 p.m.

We actually started to farm out our laboratory courses to off-site locations. In the fall of 2006 we were granted evening access from 4 p.m. to 10 p.m. to the brand-new Marine Academy of Technology and Environmental Science, one of the career academies administered by the Ocean County Vocational Technical School District. We also started to utilize several county high school laboratories in the evenings and contemplated starting laboratory hours at 6 a.m.

Microbiology had been offered as a hybrid course that OCC called an "on-site on-line" course. This did nothing to help with the laboratory space issue because the lab still had to be taught on campus. For students in the one day per week nursing program, this made an extremely long day because it had to be offered at the end of that "one day."

DECIDING TO PLACE MICROBIOLOGY TOTALLY ONLINE

The answer for our one day per week nursing students was to place microbiology totally online and have it available for students to take after they had completed two semesters of A & P or two semesters of biology as prerequisites to taking microbiology. At OCC the microbiology course was a third semester co-requisite for the nursing program, and students had to take or already have taken this course in order to progress in the nursing program. Having it available almost every semester gave students the opportunity to take it before they entered the nursing program. Many now take it over the summer so that they can concentrate on their nursing courses.

At OCC there was tremendous expertise in placing the didactic portion of a course online, but no one had figured out how to handle an online laboratory. The four-credit microbiology course had three credits dedicated to lecture and one credit dedicated to laboratory. This was the same stumbling block that we had for the A & P I and II courses. How could we place these courses totally online? Dr. Jon Larson, the visionary president of OCC, had seen a lab kit at a national conference that was used for online students. He instructed me to find out more about this "lab in a box" that came from a company in Colorado. I immediately started to investigate and found Hands-On Labs in Englewood, Colorado. They produced lab kits called LabPaqs that mirrored the experiments performed on campus laboratories across the nation and offered discipline-specific kits in a wide array of sciences. They had one specific for microbiology, which had been used for a number of years in different colleges and universities. This was the key to going forward with placing microbiology courses fully online!

I was given the opportunity to develop microbiology totally online since I had an extensive background in microbiology including a PhD in microbiology from the Waksman Institute of Microbiology at Rutgers University. My thesis was on immunosuppression and I was one of the first AIDS researchers. I have also served as the director of microbiology for Roche Biomedical Laboratories, an assistant commissioner of health for the New Jersey Department of Health and Senior Services, and a vice president and director of laboratories for the Celsis Laboratory Group. Thus, I had lots of experiences to share with online students and was excited to put microbiology totally online!

A MICROBIOLOGY LAB KIT: THE MAGIC MISSING PIECE TO THE PUZZLE

The microbiology lab kit came with everything we needed, right off the shelf. It included a full-color lab manual on a CD and contained required science equipment, chemicals, specimens, and supplies. The company also offered students an inexpensive microscope produced in India with an optional oil immersion lens that had incredibly good optics for the price. The oil immersion lens is essential for viewing bacteria. The lab kit itself was aligned nicely with our campus labs at OCC and provided a thorough microbiology laboratory experience—it was not a "Mickey Mouse" cookbook science kit! It came complete with the following experiments (Figure A.1): observing bacteria and blood, bacterial morphology, aseptic technique and culturing microbes, isolation of individual colonies, differential staining, methyl red Voges-Proskauer test, motility testing, carbohydrate fermentation testing, antibiotic sensitivity, fomite transmission, microbes in the environment, and mycology.

The kit had everything students need and utilized harmless, bio-safety level-1 organisms, which alleviated safety concerns, plus it came with a complete set of material safety data sheets (MSDS) for all its chemicals. This microbiology kit

Figure A.1.
Microbiology LabPaq Contents

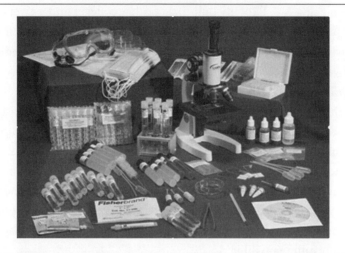

(MBK) was designed by Professor Cynthia Alonzo, who is a former research scientist and has taught microbiology for Colorado Community College Online for years. Professor Alonzo has a BS in genetics, an MS in molecular biology, and an MS in education; she designed the perfect lab kit, which fit hand in glove for us at OCC.

This kit solved a number of problems for us. Students would not have to travel to and from campus or spend money on gasoline, tolls, parking fees, insurance, and so on. Even more important they would save commuting time and be able to keep their full- or part-time jobs. They wouldn't have to pay for child care. They would have the convenience of being able to do science lab work almost anywhere and anytime. The college financial aid department could place orders online and have the kits directly shipped to the students and billed to the department. Students receiving financial aid could place their orders through our own bookstore, and the rest of the students could buy the kits online and have them shipped straight to their home.

We didn't realize it at the time, but offering microbiology and later A & P fully online opened up a niche market that was much greater than just Ocean County's students. Almost overnight out-of-state and even out-of-the-country students started taking our fully online microbiology course. It met a need nationally, and OCC found its revenues increasing due to students taking our courses from as far away as Alaska, Japan, Ireland, and Germany.

The lab kits also solved the problem of transferability. We learned from our experience placing A & P totally online that other colleges and universities would not accept a virtual science experience for transfer. They insisted that transfer courses have a hands-on laboratory experience that engaged the students in rigorous and valid science experimentation, even if it was outside a formal campus laboratory. These lab kits met this need.

Although the microbiology kit costs over $250, it includes a laboratory manual, which easily saves students around $100. The complete manual is available in digital form and can be plugged into the online course with little difficulty.

The bottom line is that the lab kit took care of the entire laboratory part of the microbiology course. I had to focus only on placing the didactic portion online and working with my students. This was the magic missing piece to the puzzle Ocean County College had been looking for, and it made placing microbiology totally online possible.

DESIGNING AND TEACHING THE MICROBIOLOGY COURSE

I was hoping to find a textbook publisher who had designed a thorough online microbiology course that I could adapt and use at OCC. No publisher-created digital content ready to use online was to my liking at the time. I decided to develop the course content from scratch and supplement it with learning objects and content tools provided by the publisher. I decided on the textbook *Microbiology: A Systems Approach,* 2nd edition, by Marjorie Cowan and Kathleen Park Talaro. The book has unique organization, an engaging writing style, and an instructional art program that really lends itself to a microbiology course with a heavy clinical focus. McGraw-Hill includes many digital tools such as animations and summaries that can be downloaded onto an MP3 player, iPod, and iPhone audio or video.

I had always loved using Dreamweaver for developing my e-learning content, but chemistry professor Maria Tamburro and Dr. Felix Rizvanov, our director of Learning Technologies with Sungard at Ocean County College, urged me to try Soft Chalk. The *Soft Chalk LessonBuilder* provides an excellent means to engage students by easily creating interactive content. I was able to create interactive learning games, including customizable flashcards, image labeling, image hotspot activities, matching games, crossword puzzles, and different question types including multiple choice, multiple answer with more than one correct answer, short answer, true/false, matching, and ordering. The pop-up text annotations help to define terminology or enhance the interactivity of the lesson content. I placed interactive content on the bottom of each page of the module to reinforce what students had just learned on that page.

A GOOD WEBSITE IS CRITICAL TO SUCCESS

It is very important to let students know what to expect in an online science course. They need to know what resources they will need before the course starts. A good website can help prepare the student. Most online courses are not accessible until the day the course starts, but this is too late for lab-based online courses. Students need to be aware right up front what the total package will cost and not be blindsided by the need to buy a lab kit and microscope equipment.

The website should include critical information for the success of the course. We put in hyperlinks to the correct lab kit and microscope as well as accessories such as the oil immersion lens that they need to order. We also have a special link for out-of-state students so that they can easily register for the course.

A huge help is the early posting of a generic syllabus. This provides out-of-state students the ability to download the entire syllabus and show it to their college administrators, who can determine whether the course will be transferable. There is also a quick tutorial and a quick test to determine if an online course is right for the student.

The website (see Figure A.2) was critical to our success and helped to reduce the number of phone calls from students needing more information. If a student inquired via e-mail, we could simply send them the URL, or web address for the website, and provide them with one-stop shopping! We also simplified the URL from www.ocean.edu/academics/programsofstudy/science/MicrobiologyOnline .htm to www.ocean.edu/micro.htm, which is a more convenient web address for students to remember and for brochures and marketing materials.

The website needs to be constantly updated to keep it accurate and fresh and to retain a high position on Google's list. Getting other sites to link to the page strengthens its position on Google and other search engines.

Ocean County College's website is now usually the first noncommercial link shown in response to a search for "microbiology online course." Fortune 500 companies pay huge sums for such a position on Google, but OCC simply acquires it from constant traffic.

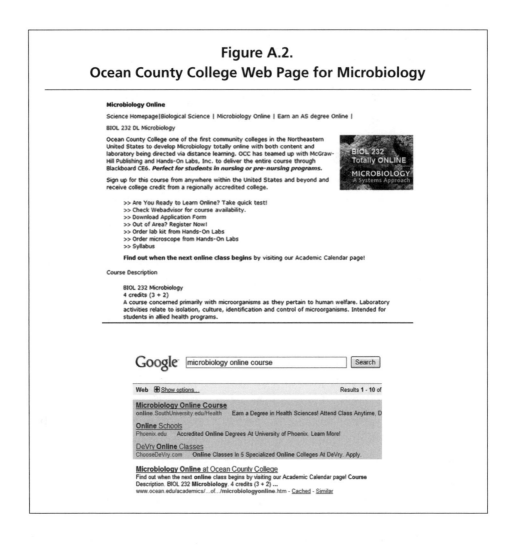

Figure A.2.
Ocean County College Web Page for Microbiology

Microbiology Online

Science Homepage|Biological Science | Microbiology Online | Earn an AS degree Online |

BIOL 232 DL Microbiology

Ocean County College one of the first community colleges in the Northeastern United States to develop Microbiology totally online with both content and laboratory being directed via distance learning. OCC has teamed up with McGraw-Hill Publishing and Hands-On Labs, Inc. to deliver the entire course through Blackboard CE6. *Perfect for students in nursing or pre-nursing programs.*

Sign up for this course from anywhere within the United States and beyond and receive college credit from a regionally accredited college.

>> Are You Ready to Learn Online? Take quick test!
>> Check Webadvisor for course availability.
>> Download Application Form
>> Out of Area? Register Now!
>> Order lab kit from Hands-On Labs
>> Order microscope from Hands-On Labs
>> Syllabus

Find out when the next online class begins by visiting our Academic Calendar page!

Course Description

BIOL 232 Microbiology
4 credits (3 + 2)
A course concerned primarily with microorganisms as they pertain to human welfare. Laboratory activities relate to isolation, culture, identification and control of microorganisms. Intended for students in allied health programs.

BIOL 232
Totally ONLINE
MICROBIOLOGY
A Systems Approach

Google [microbiology online course] [Search]

Web ⊞ Show options... Results 1 - 10 of

Microbiology Online Course
online.SouthUniversity.edu/Health Earn a Degree in Health Sciences! Attend Class Anytime, D

Online Schools
Phoenix.edu Accredited Online Degrees At University of Phoenix. Learn More!

DeVry **Online** Classes
ChooseDeVry.com Online Classes In 5 Specialized Online Colleges At DeVry. Apply.

Microbiology Online at Ocean County College
Find out when the next online class begins by visiting our Academic Calendar page! Course Description. BIOL 232 Microbiology. 4 credits (3 + 2) ...
www.ocean.edu/academics/...of.../microbiologyonline.htm - Cached - Similar

The OCC website generates significant revenue for OCC's online courses. More than half the students signing up for OCC's online microbiology course are now from out of state, and the college needs no additional lab space. This is a great example of "clicks, not bricks."

TEACHING THE MICROBIOLOGY COURSE

After the online course is built, it is necessary to actively engage students in learning. A key to successful online courses is a sense of community in the online classroom. Learning communities have restructured the classroom and formed a collaborative pedagogy that has dramatically increased student involvement, learning, and persistence. Students spend more time with their peers and more time on class matters in a cooperative and collaborative manner. Students are engaged both inside and outside their cyber-classroom, which serves to involve them more fully in the academic matters. The students see their peers and faculty as more supportive of their needs. As a result of all of this, students spend more time studying and are more engaged in the learning process. It fosters almost a foxhole frame of mind, where a we-can-get-through-this-if-we-all-stick-together attitude prevails. Creating these types of highly successful learning communities within the online classroom has been a challenge.

Breaking the Ice Online: Share Something Personal

Specific features of the course design should allow students to interact socially as well as academically. Typical of all online courses, students begin the class nervous and unsure about their ability to connect to the class site. An immediate icebreaker is the use of an introduction and photo area. My first assignment asks students to share with the class something about themselves and to provide a photo if possible. If the students are not able to provide a digital photo or scan one in, I scan it in for them. The students find a picture of the instructor with his family or pet and a paragraph about his interests, family, hobbies, pets, and so on when they begin the course. My wife, Sally, and I have six kids, three biological and three adopted. This gives me plenty to talk about as an icebreaker and encourages the students to do the same. They immediately start to bond with one another and realize that everybody new to online courses is scared to death.

The students typically respond enthusiastically to my introduction and post similar information about their lives. A "cat person" posts a number of pictures of interacting with her cat. Similarly, a "dog person" comments about the special wonder and attributes associated with his pet. This immediately sets up the sense of community similar to the one around the water cooler or in the break room in the workplace. Although many students are initially reluctant to share a picture of themselves, within the first few weeks of the course, most students have shared a personal introduction and have included a photo. After the ice is broken, students feel more comfortable discussing things of a personal nature or a personal experience related to the course topic. Swan (2002) refers to this as self-disclosure, which is defined as "the sharing of personal information, usually of a vulnerable nature." Self-disclosure is an immediacy behavior that is frequently employed by instructors to lessen the gap between themselves and their students.

Call Students If They Don't Show Up Online

When I was an assistant dean at New Jersey City University, we quickly found that it was very important for instructors to carefully monitor their courses to keep track of which students had entered the course. Further, it made a huge difference to make a telephone call to those who did not show up within the first 48 hours. The students really appreciated the call and help with managing their initial fear, and they were then more inclined to become engaged with the course rather than drop out.

The same is true with online science labs. If a student misses the first due date for the initial lab report or expresses frustration in an e-mail, I give a call and walk him or her through the process. For example, I have developed a gallery of photos for each step of the lab process to help illustrate exactly how to perform the lab and what the expected outcomes should look like; a picture is truly worth a thousand words and is a huge help to a struggling student. I found that faculty members who refused to call students and simply sent them multiple e-mails would often just frustrate instead of help the students. It is particularly critical with the online laboratory-based course to stay engaged with students and constantly monitor their progress.

Go After the "Lurkers" and Engage Them

Some people read the online discussions and postings by other students but do not participate in the discussion. These people are referred to as "lurkers." Many students have different learning styles and the lurkers may be good listeners in the face-to-face classroom and have a valid and effective learning style. They need to be treated gently by the instructor yet still be encouraged to participate. I assign a point value for attendance and participation, usually 20%. It is important to make it clear to the students exactly how they can earn these participation points.

Participation in online courses forces students to write and thereby improve their written communication skills. The major learning management systems make it easy for the online instructor to detect lurking. The instructor can easily determine what pages students have visited, how long they have visited them, and how many times each student has contributed compared to other students.

I try to give students helpful hints to improve their online communication. I have created a section where they are shown, step by step, with helpful screen shots, how to check their spelling and grammar using Microsoft Word and then paste their responses into a discussion post. I insist that spelling and grammar count no matter what subject is being taught. This really helps to reinforce the cross-curricular competency of written communication. At Ocean County College, we try to infuse "writing across the curriculum" into every course.

I deliberately use what is happening today in microbiology as a way to engage students and encourage a lively discussion on current issues. The Program for Monitoring Emerging Diseases (also known as ProMED-mail) is among the largest of publicly available emerging-disease-and-outbreak-reporting systems in the world. ProMED-mail (www.promedmail.org) publishes and transmits via the Internet an average of seven daily reports of infectious disease outbreaks with commentary from a staff of expert moderators, on a real-time basis. The students can learn about an outbreak the day before it is published in the *New York Times* and as long as two years before it appears in a textbook.

I deliberately select topics that reflect what students are learning in the course and what is happening locally. For example, Point Pleasant, a seaside community on the New Jersey shore, had many stray cats from vacationers abandoning their pets at the end of the summer. In 2009, rabies turned up in this population, and I took the opportunity to discuss this ancient disease that is still a threat today (see Figure A.3). Discussions like this help to electrify the students and motivate them to respond and continue with meaningful discussions that stimulate critical thinking and research.

Weekly discussions provide students with the opportunity to dig down and research what is happening in the world today. Depending on the complexity of the issue, at times I extend discussions over two weeks to allow follow-up questions that provide for critical thinking for further reflection.

Facilitating Courtesy, Honesty, and Respect on the Academic Playground

Students should feel as safe online as they do in their homes or with their friends. The instructor must vigilantly monitor the discussion and step in when the tone needs to be corrected. A harsh word or inappropriate statement can quickly shut down communication and destroy the sense of community. In many respects the

Figure A.3.
Ocean County College: Microbiology Discussion Board

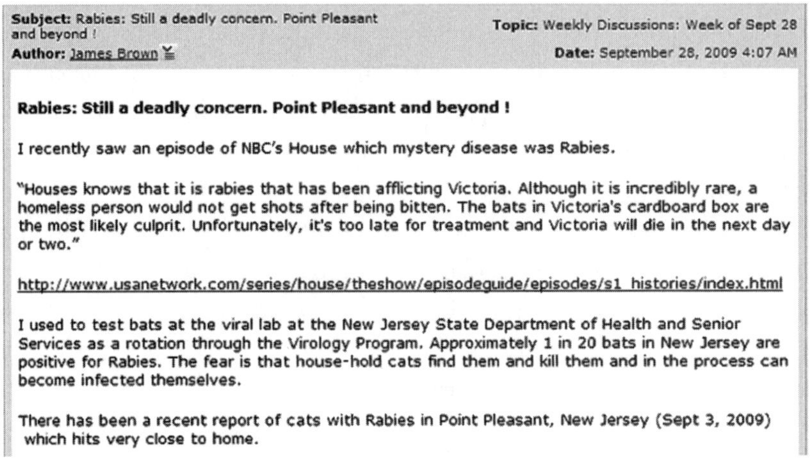

Subject: Rabies: Still a deadly concern. Point Pleasant and beyond !
Author: James Brown

Topic: Weekly Discussions: Week of Sept 28
Date: September 28, 2009 4:07 AM

Rabies: Still a deadly concern. Point Pleasant and beyond !

I recently saw an episode of NBC's House which mystery disease was Rabies.

"Houses knows that it is rabies that has been afflicting Victoria. Although it is incredibly rare, a homeless person would not get shots after being bitten. The bats in Victoria's cardboard box are the most likely culprit. Unfortunately, it's too late for treatment and Victoria will die in the next day or two."

http://www.usanetwork.com/series/house/theshow/episodeguide/episodes/s1_histories/index.html

I used to test bats at the viral lab at the New Jersey State Department of Health and Senior Services as a rotation through the Virology Program. Approximately 1 in 20 bats in New Jersey are positive for Rabies. The fear is that house-hold cats find them and kill them and in the process can become infected themselves.

There has been a recent report of cats with Rabies in Point Pleasant, New Jersey (Sept 3, 2009) which hits very close to home.

---

instructor acts as a playground monitor, allowing students to interact cooperatively with one another to build creations in the virtual sandbox.

Instructors are responsible for creating an atmosphere of inclusion and safety where participants can speak and debate their ideas without fear of retribution or destructive criticism. I will quietly address students with a private and confidential e-mail or even a phone call if they are not adhering to the principles of netiquette. I have an entire web page describing the principles of netiquette; it outlines the expectations for students' online conduct: to always be appropriate and courteous to other Internet users.

Monitoring the Laboratory Work

I use a separate drop box for students to submit their laboratory reports and try to give them a few weeks to get their lab kits ordered and to get comfortable with their microscope equipment. Some students avoid ordering a lab kit because they want to save money or they think they can cheat and use information on the Internet to fudge a report. I make sure that the students actually purchase a kit and the microscope by placing this statement right in the syllabus:

> You *must* purchase a LabPaq and microscope to complete this
> course—failure to do so will be considered cheating and you will

either be withdrawn from this course or, in the worst case scenario, receive a failing grade. In order to pass this course, all labs must be completed with a combined average score of at least a 70.

I obtain a list of students who purchased lab kits for my course from the kit company and verify that all students actually obtained one.

I also encourage students to purchase a digital eyepiece microscope camera attachment to take pictures of what they are seeing under the microscope. Hands-On Labs offers a very affordable one. It comes with an adapter that connects the microscope directly to a computer through a USB port so that students can download pictures of what they see.

I also ask students to take pictures of themselves performing the labs plus close-up shots of their culture test tubes, culture plates, reagent tubes that turn colors after incubating, and so on. (See examples in Figures A.4 and A.5.) This gives me assurance they are doing the laboratory work and alerts me if they are having difficulty because I can see what they are doing and help them troubleshoot any problems. Some students who are not very adept at digital photography use their cell phones to take the picture. Whether or not the photography is worthy of an award, it helps me to monitor the work being done.

Figure A.4.
Streak Plate with Staphylococcus Epidermis Isolated

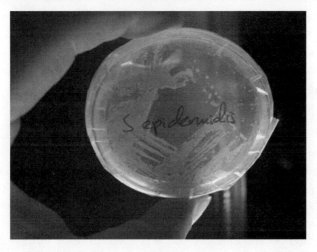

Courtesy of OCC student Jason Driggars

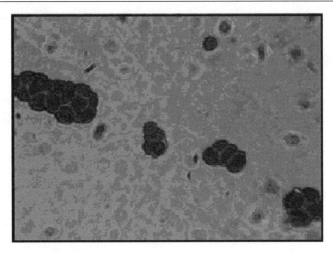

Figure A.5.
Saccharomyces Cerevisiae, a Budding Yeast

Courtesy of OCC student Jason Driggars

I also ask students to include a colored-pencil sketch to illustrate their lab work. (See Figure A.6.) Some students scan these in and send them along rather than submitting a digital photo. Paint is a simple graphics drawing program that is included with all versions of Microsoft Windows. It opens and saves files as Windows bitmap, JPEG, GIF, PNG, and TIFF files. The program can be in color mode or black-and-white, but there is no grayscale mode. Students make surprisingly wonderful images that they send along with their lab reports.

Student Feedback

Student feedback on OCC's online microbiology course is overwhelmingly positive. Students uniformly feel a tremendous sense of accomplishment for being able to master the online microbiology course. They find the lab kits to be fun, enlightening, and exciting. Comments like "the experiments really work" and "I couldn't believe I could do it" are very common. Here are some other comments:

> This really was an enjoyable and very interesting step into becoming a nurse. I personally thought the labs were entertaining, and made

---
Figure A.6.
Gram Stain Illustration

Experiment 5: Differential Staining

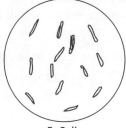 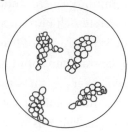

E. Coli
Geam − Stained Red/Pink

S. Epidermidis
Geam + − Stained Purple

Courtesy of OCC student Umar Khawaja

---

me focus and learn about what I growing and swabbing. Also the weekly discussion board had some very interesting topics that were very beneficial to my learning. Also, thank you for responding to my e-mails and calls!! Your patience was appreciated.

Thanks for such a fun class—I really enjoyed the labs and the practical applications to the material! I can't believe this class is almost over, I'm enjoying every minute!

Thank you so much! I learned so much more here, online, than I ever would have in a classroom during the summer. Being online really made me pay attention more and actually learn the material for myself. You have been such a great help. Thanks again.

Sponges Versus Coral in the Online Sea

Rena Palloff and Keith Pratt (2007) use the analogy of the sponge versus the coral with respect to building community in online courses. The sponge is content to simply sit still and soak up the nutrients in its environment without making any contribution to the surrounding ecosystem. Some students in online courses initially behave as sponges, taking in the wealth of the course but contributing little. On the other hand and with encouragement, the vast majority of students can become like corals, the building platform for a thriving undersea ecosystem. Corals protect, support, and strengthen the entire ecosystem and add new layers to that which existed before. The coral is analogous to the optimum online community where students and instructor support and protect one another and all secrete rich nutrients to encourage the growth of knowledge and to support the delicate process of learning.

Using techniques to build community online has resulted in retention rates of 95% or greater, considerably higher than the 70–75% national average for online courses. Teaching microbiology totally online is a challenging yet extremely rewarding experience. LabPaqs were the key to the success of OCC's course. In addition to adopting the microbiology lab kit, OCC also adopted A & P I and II lab kits for its nursing students. It then went further, put its entire science program online with lab kits, and has continued its success with offering lab science courses completely online.

OCC students continue to learn and master difficult material. They find that they enjoy learning and being actively involved in the inquiry-based science laboratory investigations. They find their fellow students to be reliable, trusted resources. Together, OCC's instructors and students enjoy a rich and productive learning environment. And together they are building a stronger, more robust coral reef.

REFERENCES

Allen, E., & Seaman, J. (2008). *Staying the course: Online education in the United States, 2008.* Sloan Consortium sixth annual report. Needham, MA: Sloan-C.

American Chemical Society (ACS). (2009, September 1). Position statement on computer simulations in academic laboratories. Retrieved from http://portal.acs.org/portal/acs/corg/content?_nfpb=true&_pageLabel=PP_SUPERARTICLE&node_id=2223&use_sec=false&sec_url_var=region1&__uuid=

Bradley, M. (2008). *Innovative online A&P course with "wet lab" that delivers better results than face-to-face courses.* Presentation workshop given at the Human Anatomy and Physiology Society conference in New Orleans, LA, May 20, 2008.

Brown, J. W. (2009a, May 22). *Brave new world: Putting science courses totally online.* Presented at the University of Denver Spring Symposium, Denver, CO.

Brown, J. W. (2009b, January). *Running out of science laboratory space on your campus? Put science totally online!* Presented at Educause Learning Imitative Conference: Social Learning for the 21st Century, Orlando, FL.

Brown, J., LaBella, M., Bradley, M., & Spenser, C. (2007, November 8). *Brave new world: Teaching anatomy & physiology totally online.* Presented at the 13th Sloan Consortium (Sloan-C) International Conference on Online Learning, Orlando, FL.

Brown, J. W., LaBella, M., Bradley, M., Tamburro, M., Spencer, C., & Rizvanov, F. (2009, March 22). *Putting science courses totally online.* Presented at the Sungard Summit Connect 2009 Conference, Toms River, NJ.

Bushweller, K. 1999. "Generation of Cheaters." *The American School Board Journal,* April. Online: www.asbj.com/199904/0499coverstory.html

Cantor, J. A. (1996). *Experiential learning in higher education: Linking classroom and community.* Retrieved from National Teaching & Learning Forum website: http://www.ntlf.com/html/lib/bib/95–7dig.htm

Carnevale, D. (2002, November 12). Baking soda, vinegar, and measuring cups become lab materials for online chemistry course. *Chronicle of Higher Education.* Retrieved from http://chronicle.com/free/2002/11/2002111201t.htm

Carter, D. (2009, October 26). Online courses often pricier for students. *eSchool News.* Retrieved from http://www.eschoolnews.com/news/top-news/index.cfm?i=61405

Cavanaugh, C., Gillan, K. J., Kromrey, J., Hess, M., & Blomeyer, R. (2004.) *The effects of distance education on K–12 student outcomes: A meta-analysis.* Naperville, IL: Learning Point Associates. Retrieved from http://www.ncrel.org/tech/distance/index.html

CCCOnline. (2008, April). CCCOnline celebrating 10th anniversary with record enrollments. *Colorado Community College Connections, 4*(1). Retrieved from http://www.cccs.edu/communications/connections/2008/april/page2.html

Center for Science, Mathematics, and Engineering Education (CSMEE), National Research Council. (1996). *National science education standards.* Washington, DC: National Academies Press. Retrieved from http://www.nap.edu/catalog.php?record_id=4962

Chenobu, V. (2007, May). *Online chemistry experiments.* Presented at the SUNY regional conference, Platteville, NY.

Chisholm, J. K. (2006). Pleasure and danger in online teaching and learning. *Academe, 92*(6), 39–42.

Christian, W., & Belloni, M. (2001). *Physlets: Teaching physics with interactive curricular material.* Upper Saddle River, NJ: Prentice Hall.

Duncan, T. (2009, April). Expanding opportunities for teaching college lab science courses fully online. Presented at the annual TxDLA conference, Corpus Christi, TX.

Feynman, R. P. (1964). *The Feynman lectures on physics.* Reading, MA: Addison-Wesley.

Frederickson, N., Reed, P., & Clifford, V. (2005). Evaluating web-supported learning versus lecture based teaching: Quantitative and qualitative perspectives. *Higher Education, 50*(4), 645–664.

Frese, J. (2006). *Handbook for online faculty.* Unpublished manuscript, Fresno City College.

George. (2009, June 29). From a student's perspective [Online forum comment]. Retrieved from http://www.insidehighered.com/news/2009/06/29/online#Comments

Gibson-Brown, R. (2010, April 9). *Teaching biology fully online is now a reality: Don't reinvent the wheel.* Presented at the Association of Southeastern Biologists Conference in Asheville, NC.

Green, K. C. (2009). Executive summary. *Managing online education programs: The 2009 WCET (Western Cooperative for Educational Telecommunications) and Campus Computing Project survey.* Retrieved from http://wcet.wiche.edu/wcet/docs/moe/ManagingOnlineEd2009-ExecSummary.pdf (summarized in a sponsor-briefing webcast at the WCET Annual Conference. Retrieved from http://wiche.edu/attachment_library/ManagingOnlineEducation/MANAGINGONLINEED-SESSIONGRAPHICS.pdf)

Gutman, H. F. (1940). The life of Ira Ramsen. *Journal of Chemical Education, 17.*

Hands-On Labs (HOL). (2009). *LabPaq student survey, May 2009.* Retrieved from http://www.labpaq.com/files/Student%20Survey%20SumComments_D_0509.doc

Herzog, J. (2008, November). *Innovative techniques for teaching a hands-on lab course over the Internet*. Online presentation at the Internet Academy of Herkimer County Community College. Retrieved from http://www.labpaq.com/docs/JenHerzog-PRESENTATION2.ppt

Ittelson, J. (2009, October 29). Towards a sustainable approach to higher education. *Campus Technology Online Journal*. Retrieved from http://campustechnology.com/articles/2009/10/28/towards-a-sustainable-approach-to-higher-education.aspx

Jang, K. S., Hwang, S. Y., Park, S. J., Kim, Y. M., & Kim, M. J. (2005). Effects of a web-based teaching method on undergraduate nursing students' learning of electrocardiography. *The Journal of Nursing Education, 44*(1), 35–39.

Jaschik, S. (2009, June 29). The evidence on online education. *Inside Higher Ed.* Retrieved from http://www.insidehighered.com/news/2009/06/29/online

Jeschofnig, P. (1992a). *Experiential education in hydrology at Colorado Mountain College*. Paper presented at the annual Water Resources and Environment Conference, Fort Collins, CO.

Jeschofnig, P. (1992b). *Experiential learning in environmental sciences*. Paper presented at the Conference of the National Society of Internship and Experiential Education, Newport, RI.

Jeschofnig, P. (2004, August). *Effective laboratory experiences for distance learning science courses with self-contained laboratory kit*. Presented at the 20th Annual Conference on Distance Teaching and Learning, Madison, WI.

Jeschofnig, P. (2006, November 6). *We teach, but are they learning*. Presented at the 12th annual Sloan-C Conference, Orlando, FL.

Jeschofnig, P. (2009, March). Challenges and solutions for online lab science courses. Presented at the League of Innovations Conference, Reno, NV. Retrieved from http://www.league.org/iStreamSite/content/ppt/inv2009/S439.ppt#256.1.Challenges&SolutionsforOnlineLabScienceCourses

Jeschofnig, P., & Spencer, C. (2008, November 5–7). *Success in online vs. on-campus lab science courses*. Presented at the 14th annual Sloan-C Conference, Orlando, FL.

Kearns, S. P., Kelly, A. L., Barrett, J., Schlossbach, N., Quinn, M., Olsen, C., Keenan, C., Brewer, L., & J. W. Brown. (2006). The one day per week nursing program: A web-assisted associate degree nursing program. *Teaching and Learning in Nursing, 1*(1), 10–17.

Kleiner, C., & Lord, M. (1999, November 2). The cheating game: "Everyone's doing it," from grade school to graduate school. *U.S. News & World Report,* 55–66.

Kolowich, S. (2009, October 22). Online education's great unknowns. *Inside Higher Ed.* Retrieved from http://www.insidehighered.com/news/2009/10/22/online

Lamb, G. M. (2009, October 15). The future of college may be virtual. *Christian Science Monitor*. Retrieved from http://features.csmonitor.com/innovation/2009/10/15/the-future-of-college-may-be-virtual

Lupton, R. A., Chapman, K. J., & Weiss, J. E. (2000). A cross-national exploration of business students' attitudes, perceptions, and tendencies toward academic dishonesty. *Journal of Education for Business, 75*(4), 231–235.

Lyall, R., & Patti, A. F. (2010). *Taking the chemistry experience home—Home experiments or "kitchen chemistry" in accessible elements: Teaching science online and at a distance.* Athabaska, AB: Athabaska University Press.

Maeroff, G. I. (2003). *A classroom of one: How online learning is changing our schools and colleges.* Basingstoke, UK: Palgrave MacMillan.

Means, B., Toyama, Y., Murphy, R., Bakla, M., & Jones, K. (2009). *Evaluation of evidence-based practices in online learning: A meta-analysis and review of online learning studies.* U.S. Department of Education, Office of Planning, Evaluation, and Policy Development, Policy and Program Studies Service. Retrieved from http://www.ed.gov/rschstat/eval/tech/evidence-based-practices/finalreport.pdf

Mentzer, G. A., Cryan, J., & Teclehaimanot, B. (2007). A comparison of face-to-face and web-based classrooms. *Journal of Technology and Teacher Education, 15*(2), 233–246.

Mishra, P., & Koehler, M. (2006). Technological pedagogical content knowledge: A framework for teacher knowledge. *Teachers College Record, 108*(6), 1017–1054.

Mooney, C., & Kirshenbaum, S. (2009). *Unscientific America: How scientific illiteracy threatens our future.* New York, NY: Basic Books.

Nagel, D. (2009, October 28). Most college students to take classes online by 2014. *Campus Technology Online Journal.* Retrieved from http://campustechnology.com/articles/2009/10/28/most-college-students-to-take-classes-online-by-2014.aspx

National Science Teachers Association (NSTA). (2009, April). *Position statement: The integral role of laboratory investigations in science instruction.* Retrieved from http://www.nsta.org/about/positions/laboratory.aspx

National Society for Experiential Education (NSEE). (1998). *Standards of practice: Eight principles of good practice for all experiential learning activities.* Presented at the 1998 NSEE Annual Meeting, Norfolk, VA.

Palloff, R., & Pratt, K. (2007). *Building learning communities in cyberspace: Effective strategies for the online classroom* (2nd ed.). San Francisco, CA: Jossey-Bass.

Perkins-Johnston, P. S. (2010, January). *Change has come—Now you can teach lab-based science fully online.* Presented at the Association for Science Teacher Education Conference, Sacramento, CA.

Rice University Laboratory Educators in Natural Sciences and Engineering. (2006). Brief list of program-wide teaching and learning objectives. *Interdisciplinary web-based teaching laboratory material.* Retrieved from http://www.owlnet.rice.edu/~labgroup/assessment/lab_objectives.html

Shachar, M., & Neumann, Y. (2010). Twenty years of research on the academic performance differences between traditional and distance learning: Summative meta-analysis and trend examination. *MERLOT Journal of Online Learning and Teaching, 6*(2). Retrieved from http://jolt.merlot.org/vol6no2/shachar_0610.htm

SL. (2009, June 29). It's called accountability . . . [Online forum comment]. Retrieved from http://www.insidehighered.com/news/2009/06/29/online#Comments

Standler, R. B. (2000). *Plagiarism in colleges in USA*. Retrieved from http://www.rbs2 .com/plag.htm

Stuber-McEwen, D., Wiselye, P., & Hoggartt, S. (2009, Fall). Point, click, and cheat: Frequency and type of academic dishonesty in the virtual classroom. *Online Journal of Distance Learning Administration* (University of West Georgia, Distance Education Center), *12*(3).

Swan, K. (2002). Building learning communities in online courses: The importance of interaction. *Education, Communication and Information, 2*(1), 23–27.

Taylor, I. (2009, June 28). Online learning is gaining credibility. *Richmond Times Dispatch*. Retrieved from http://www.timesdispatch.com/rtd/business/columnists/ article/IRIS28_20090627-184803/276776/

Teachout, Z. (2009, September 8). Welcome to Yahoo! U: The web will dismember universities, just like newspapers. *The Big Money*. Retrieved from http://www .thebigmoney.com/articles/diploma-mill/2009/09/08/welcome-yahoo-u

Thompson, P. (2010, March). *Online learning comes to lab sciences—Don't re-invent the wheel*. Presented at the Texas Community College Teachers Association, Dallas, TX.

Vass, L. (2007, November 9). Anatomy and physiology: It's not just on campus anymore! Presented at the 13th annual Sloan-C Conference, Orlando, FL.

Vorndam, M. (2007, February). Survey of online student satisfaction and learning at CCC-Online asking students' lab preference. Presented at the ITC e-Learning Conference, Albuquerque, NM.

Wherry, P. S., & Lundberg, D. (2009). When distance technologies meet the student code. In D. Gearhart (Ed.), *Cases on distance delivery and learning outcomes: Emerging trends and programs*. Hershey, PA: Information Science Reference.

Woodfield, B., Catlin, H. R., Waddoups, G. L., Moore, M. S., Swan, R., Allen, R., & Bodily, G. (2004, November 1). The Virtual ChemLab project: A realistic and sophisticated simulation of inorganic qualitative analysis. *Journal of Chemistry Education, 81*(11), 1672.

INDEX

Chat rooms, 40

Cheating, 86–87, 93; dishonesty, eliminating, 92; on lab work/lab reports, 92–94; tools to prevent/ reduce, 88–92

Chemical Thesaurus, 46

Chenobu, V., 19, 21, 31, 76

Chisholm, J. K., 22

Christian, W., 108

Clifford, V., 31

Colorado Mountain College, 65, 125–126

Commercially assembled lab kits, 61–64, 110–116; adoption process, 116; anatomy kits, 111–112; commercial lab kit suppliers, selecting, 112–114; cost of, 62; dissections, 112; eScience Labs, 62, 113; evidence supporting the effectiveness of, 64–65; by Hands-On Labs (HOL), 62; LabPaq titration experiment, 111; manuals, 110; microbiology kits, 111; ordering, 114–115; and physical engagement of students in active learning, 63–64; physics kits, 111; as substitutes for traditional lab sessions, 63

Computer capabilities, 69

Computer simulations, 100–108; Bacterial Identification Lab, The, 104; Biology Labs Online, 104, 106; Bioquest, 106; Model Science Software, 104; Neurophysiology Lab, The, 104; PhET, 106–107; PhysicsLab, 107; PhysicsLessons.com iPhysics, 107; Physlets, 107–108; as post-labs, 101–103; as pre-labs, 101–103; shortcomings, 101–102; as substitutes for expensive/dangerous experiments, 102; as substitutes for traditional lab experiences, 52; Virtual Chemistry Experiments (Davidson College), 105; Virtual ChemLab projects

(Woodfield), 103, 105; Virtual Physics Laboratory, 107; Virtual Pig, 106–107

Cookbooking, 101

Courses: activities and design, 69–70; calendar, 70; content discussions, 78–79; description, 68; equipment, 69; information, 68; materials, 69

Course management system (CMS), *See* Learning management system (LMS)

Cowan, M., 152

Credit hours, 68

Cryan, J., 31

Curriculum-development tools, 39

D

Desire2Learn, 38

Diigo, 42–43

DimDim, 41–42

Discussion boards, 19–20, 76–83; chat, 83; general course, 77–82; lab, 82; personal interaction with an instruction, benefits of, 20; participation, 71–72; purposes served by, 19; rubric for assessment of required weekly postings to, 79

Distant online students, 8

Drop policy, 72–73

Duncan, T., 31

E

eLearning Network, 44

Elluminate, 41

eScience Labs, 62, 113

F

Facebook, 43–44

Feynman, R. P., 6

L

M

N

Neurophysiology Lab, The, 104
Nontraditional students: and online courses, 14

O

Obstacles to teaching science online, 22–24; belief in ability to teach/learn lab sciences in online format, 31–32; communication, 34–35; confidence, 28; cost of online course development, 28–29; instructor's time, 23–26; liability, 29–31; politics, 27–28; pre-semester investment of time, 32–34; transfer of credits, 26

Ocean County College (OCC), 24–25, 123–125, *See also* Microbiology course at OCC; administrative challenges, 148; decision to move microbiology online, 149–150; Hands-On Labs (HOL), 150; laboratory space issue, 148–149; material safety data sheets (MSDS), 150; microbiology courses online, 147–162; microbiology lab kit, 150–152; moving a lab science course to online delivery, time required for, 24–25; niche market, creation of, 151–152; ODPW nursing program, 148; teaching the microbiology course online, 154–162; website, 153–154

Off-campus science labs: Colorado Mountain College, 125–126; evidence supporting, 121–127; Herkimer County Community College (SUNY), 126–127; Ocean County College (OCC), 123–125

Olsen, C., 148

Online cheating, 86–87; *See also* Cheating

Online communication: meaningfulness of, 19–20; one-to-one and F2 live communication compared to, 18; time lags/delays, 18–19

Online courses: and adult women students, 14; belief in, 31–32; compared to on-campus courses, 17–18; content, adding visual learning content to, 74–75; cost of developing, 28–29; demand for, 13–14; discussion boards, 19–20; dramatic rise in demand for, 13–14; and effective communication, 21; features, adding, 22; getting approvals, 25–26; instructor availability, 32–34; instructor communication, 34–35; instructor confidence, 28; instructor's time, 23–26; and international students, 15; laboratory, 20–21; and laid-off workers, 14–15; liability, 29–31; and military personnel, 15; overcoming obstacles to teaching, 22–23; politics, 27; privacy provided by, 21; and rural students, 15; and traditional college students, 15; transfer credits, 26

Online education: demand for, 13–15; move to, 11–12

Online Educator, 44

Online hours, 68

Online instruction, effectiveness of, 27–28

Online lab assignments, incorporating, 99–120

Online lab-science course, enrollment in, 20

Online quizzes and exams, 72

Online response times, 68

Online science courses, *See also* Obstacles to teaching science online; art of teaching, 67–83; bias against, 145; commercial lab kits, using with, 110–116; computer simulations, 100–108; discussion boards, 76–83; instructor-assembled lab kits, using, 108–110; interactive presentations, 74–76; kitchen labs, using,

More Resources from the Jossey-Bass Online Teaching and Learning Series!

The Essential Online Teaching and Learning Tool Kit
ISBN: 1118027213 | Price: $105.00 USD

Online teaching and learning is expanding rapidly on campuses everywhere, yet educators often lack the resources they need to translate their courses to an online environment. We've taken the guesswork out of assembling the professional development library you need, offering hand-picked resources that cover all of your online teaching and learning needs.

Tool kit includes:

Learning In Real Time by Jonathan E. Finkelstein

Engaging the Online Learner by Rita-Marie Conrad and J. Ana Donaldson

Assessing the Online Learner by Rena M. Palloff and Keith Pratt

Conquering the Content by Robin M. Smith

Creating a Sense of Presence Online by Rosemary M. Lehman and Simone C. O. Conceicao

> **You save 25%**
> on **all titles** when you buy the complete tool kit!

Join The Jossey-Bass Online Teaching and Learning Community!

The Jossey-Bass Online Teaching and Learning (OTL) Conference ONLINE
Based on the popular series of Jossey-Bass guide-books on online teaching and learning, the OTL Conference Online brings all of the books' authors – as well as a community of hundreds of professionals worldwide – right to your desktop for interactive online sessions, discussions, hands-on learning, strategy swapping, and networking. The conference takes place every October, so mark your calendars in advance!

The Jossey-Bass OTL Community Website
The learning continues all year round at the Jossey-Bass OTL community website. You'll be the first to know about details of the upcoming OTL conference, receive information on the newest professional development resources from Jossey-Bass, learn about the latest free podcasts and video clips from your favorite authors and experts, and discover much more! You can also sign up for the *OTL Update*, a FREE monthly e-newsletter full of the latest tips and tricks from experts in the field – just visit the site and sign up today!

Join our community and be the first to know about the final dates and details of our next OTL Conference Online by visiting **www.onlineteachingandlearning.com**.